To Isabel — with

Ordination to the Pr[...]

December 17ᵗʰ 1994.

Joan.

The Fire and the Clay

Also by George Guiver CR *and published by SPCK:*

Company of Voices: Daily Prayer and the People of God (1988)
Faith in Momentum: The Distinctiveness of the Church (1990)

The Fire and the Clay:

The Priest in Today's Church

Peter Allan CR

Christopher Gray

Jonathan Greener

George Guiver CR

David Peebles

Christopher Seville

First published in Great Britain 1993
Society for Promoting Christian Knowledge
Holy Trinity Church
Marylebone Road
London NW1 4DU

© Peter Allan CR, Christopher Gray, Jonathan Greener, George
Guiver CR, David Peebles, Christopher Seville 1993

All rights reserved. No part of this book may be reproduced or
transmitted in any form or by any means, electronic or
mechanical, including photocopying, recording, or by any
information storage and retrieval system, without permission in
writing from the publisher.

British Library Cataloguing-in-Publication Data
A catalogue record for this book is available from the British
Library

ISBN 0–281–04715–4

Typeset by Parker Typesetting Service, Leicester
Printed in Great Britain by
The Cromwell Press Ltd, Melksham, Wiltshire

. . . thou art fire, sacred and hallow'd fire
And I but earth and clay . . .

George Herbert

CONTENTS

The authors   ix

Acknowledgements   x

Introduction   1

PART ONE

1. Who is the 'real me'?   5

2. How do we belong?   18

3. Who is the priest?   41

PART TWO

4. Types of knowing   69

5. Till Christ be formed in you   74

6. Life together   89

7. Learning and the love of God   99

8. Being a pastor   110

9. Shaping the shepherds   128

10. Three encounters   137

THE AUTHORS

Peter Allan CR
Director of Studies, College of the Resurrection, Mirfield

Christopher Gray
College of the Resurrection 1989–92; Curate, St Jude,
Stockbridge Village / Cantril Farm, Liverpool

Jonathan Greener
College of the Resurrection 1989–91; Curate, St Matthew,
The Elephant and Castle

George Guiver CR
Vice-Principal, College of the Resurrection, Mirfield

David Peebles
College of the Resurrection 1988–90; Curate, St Andrew,
Crewe

Christopher Seville
College of the Resurrection 1987–89; Curate, Holy Nativity,
Knowle, Bristol

ACKNOWLEDGEMENTS

Our thanks are due to SPCK for encouraging our project, and among those who read and commented on the manuscript we are particularly grateful to Silvanus Berry CR, Jackie Birdseye, Stephen Brown, Paul Evans, Angus Galbraith, Benedict Green CR, Sonia Gregger, Alan Jones SDB, Doris Joy, Lance Marsden, Victor Parsons, Gary Stevens, Margaret Turk, Christine Warrilow, Monica Weld-Richards, and David Wylie, and also to Christopher Irvine for some thoughts in Chapter 5. We are also grateful to Cecily Boulding OP and Helmut Steinlein for their contributions to Chapter 9.

INTRODUCTION

This book is an organic work, the fruit of some intense labour by a group who share a common experience and vision in six distinctive forms. We started work in January 1993 and by the end of March the manuscript was with the publisher. We could meet only three times, but the nature of the exercise was to work fast and intensely to sustain momentum and complete the job while the brew of our interaction was still fresh. Being very busy people, this was quite a challenge, something which at moments we have almost been moved to regret taking on. In the event we reached a point something like the one we had in our sights, and have some hope that it will be of help both to parish clergy and layfolk and also to all concerned with the training of the clergy.

The book is about Christian priesthood. In Part One we look at certain fundamentals: what it means to be a human person; what is meant by the Church, and how priesthood fits within that context; and finally to the heart of the matter: what exactly do we mean when we speak of certain Christians being priests?

In Part Two we go on to examine four cardinal aspects of the priest's life, and in the process we take a look at ordination training – how it is, and how it needs to be. In all of this a picture emerges of certain aspects of Christian ministry which are easily obscured or forgotten in our modern age. We believe the resulting picture is a compelling and to some extent sur-prising one. It is indeed 'certain aspects' with which the book deals: it is not a compendium on the priesthood. Not all matters of pressing importance are examined. We have said little about marriage and priesthood, and we have not directly addressed the question of the ordination of women to the priesthood – not least because all shades of opinion on this matter are represented among us. But we hope to have given a coherent picture which will stimulate further reflection.

It will probably help the reader to know in advance that each chapter is preceded by a story (all the characters and situations here are fictional). This gives a continuous alternation between the experience of parish life and reflection upon it. The stories do not always connect directly with the chapters which follow, but operate sometimes as foils, sometimes as starting-points. We hope they will give both pleasure and assistance in coming to grips with a subject which is both earthy and at the same time a teaser.

Each chapter is the fruit of group work, making this more than simply a collection of essays. A general responsibility for particular chapters was distributed as follows: 1 Peter Allan, 2 and 5 George Guiver, 3 Christopher Gray, 6 David Peebles, 7 Christopher Seville, 8 Jonathan Greener.

Readers may find the first chapter a demanding start, but we ask them to persevere, as we found the question 'Who are we as human persons?' the inevitable starting-point.

PART ONE

CHAPTER ONE

Who is the 'real me'?

The door opened and there stood a big, forceful woman who in a quick look took in the whole situation.

'Kevin! Come in. This is nice to see you so soon.'

Down the cluttered passage into the chaotic kitchen.

'Tea or coffee? Well what have we done to deserve this so soon after your ordination?'

By now she was speaking with a cigarette waggling from her lips while she fixed up the kettle.

'I'm working my way through the electoral roll,' said Kevin, wondering what he was going to be in for this time.

'How does it feel after just three days? I must say I don't envy you your job.'

Now Kath had a bone of contention, and didn't spare much time in getting to the point. 'You won't have come across my niece Beverley – Tony wouldn't christen her baby, you know.'

'Well,' said Kevin, 'it's a bit more complicated than that', and as best as he could he gave the routine explanation.

'But you clergy are all the same – the Church has no need to be so stolid and stuffy about things – I think the clergy live in a world of their own sometimes.'

Kevin, who was not a particularly patient person, began to feel the blood rise in his neck.

'I don't know you very well yet, Kevin, but I hope you won't get like most of the clergy become – we need priests who stay natural and don't get stuck up there on a high horse.'

Kevin made his way back through the park to try and cool off. *Why am I suddenly assumed to represent the institution, to be it? Four days ago I was just ordinary Kev in a sweater and jeans. What will this job turn me into? I have already had to learn to tone down some of my ways, things which I thought were typical me, after that embarrassing evening at the pub with the churchwardens. I suddenly feel so official.*

The following week's Post-Ordination Training session was a desultory morning meeting in a country vicarage. There was no shortage of things to complain about, and Kevin got his bit in about not being sure who he was any more – he seemed to be having to re-model himself to other people's expectations. That started off a round of stories about a matter that had filled others with unease too.

'That's nothing to what it's like for me,' said Alison from St Mary Magdalen's. 'My problem is not being sure what is expected of me, and it's not always easy to see what belongs to the deacon and what belongs to man's way of doing things.'

A couple of weeks later Kevin preached for the first time. Kath sidled up to him over coffee afterwards. 'How's it going, Kevin? Settling in, are you?'

Then she puzzled him initially by asking, 'Have you lived abroad at all? I just wondered if you had been in Africa or somewhere.'

'Well, I've travelled a bit in Europe, but never further than that.'

'Oh – I just wondered – because when people go out there they often talk down to the people as if they were children. I just thought you might have been abroad.'

He almost dropped his coffee, and didn't pick himself up off the floor for the rest of the day. *People haven't the slightest idea how vulnerable you are straight after preaching a sermon.* He was going to have to live with that. *But people were also sniffing out that the old Kev wasn't good enough, and he was lucky, he supposed,* trying his hardest to be philosophical about it as he ate his lonely Sunday dinner, *that some of it was coming before his face and not all going behind his back.*

He became much more cheerful at the youth club that evening

when one of the helpers, Marion, thought his sermon was hysterical, and got him laughing at it. 'Give over with all that stuff,' she said, 'give us the real Kev.'

This book is about what it is to be a priest. It is written for priests and ordinands, for those who prepare others for ordination to the priesthood, and for Christians today who are not sure that there is a difference between the priest and other ministers of the gospel. There is a good deal of confusion about. Some appear to think that priests are simply the managers of the church or that priesthood is a professional calling like other caring roles. As a result we are unable to recognize what kind of preparation and formation is needed; we are not clear what to expect of a priest; and priests are confused by the many conflicting expectations that confront them. Although it has not always seemed so in the past, priests are clearly human – they are real people. Indeed, we can say that to be a priest is one distinctive way of being a human person. Further, priesthood does not stand on its own. At ordination the candidate is given a Bible, frequently inscribed by the bishop: '. . . ordained a priest *in the Church of God*'. Priests are 'stewards of the mysteries of God'. They belong within the Church. They live in the world amongst those who believe and those who do not. At the same time they are to be at home in the world of God which is infinitely greater than our physical universe. Part of our difficulty in understanding the priesthood lies in our struggle to understand our world and ourselves and the God whom we worship. If we are to appreciate the distinctive life of the priest we must first look at the way we live in the world, coming to terms with ourselves, with others and with God. We must ask what we mean by the 'real me'.

In search of the real me

A changing world

We do not live in a static environment, but in a world of change. When we say that the world has changed, we mean many things.

We are recognizing that the physical structure of things is constantly changing. A mountain may look as though it has always been there, yet we know there is constant movement and change even in such massive and seemingly permanent rock structures. We are also acknowledging that our understanding of things is changing. We have today a language for talking about the nature of the universe that is quite different from that of our ancestors a thousand years ago. In the development of the human sciences we have ways of speaking about ourselves which have profoundly affected the way we live. When we talk of the world changing we also want to say something of our experience in the last one hundred and fifty years when the rate of change has exceeded our wildest imagining.

In the last century, as new discoveries burst upon the scene day after day, there was a powerful optimism that embraced the change and saw it as development and progress. Little of that remains. More characteristically, we are the generation that lives with the awareness that we have the capacity to destroy the world as we know it. The technology of communication has given us instant access to every corner of the globe and we see and grieve over the destruction that surrounds us. The knowledge and sight that the television camera brings us are painful. We are often overcome with a sense of helplessness and futility. Our excitement at new technological advances is tempered by our squandering of the earth's resources.

A mystery to ourselves

The changes are real, but they cannot conceal an unchanging truth. Being human, in the midst of all this, is a mystery. We are conscious of contradictions that have been recorded by men and women from the beginning. At the heart is a sense of freedom; we believe in our freedom. And yet, it seems, this freedom is not enough, for we cannot prevent destruction. Or, worse, this sense of freedom is illusory: we are instead bound into a chain of events over which we have no real control. Discussion of the nature and character of human freedom is not, of course, confined to consideration of our relationship to the material world. It refers equally to our relationships with other persons, and indeed with ourselves. We can sometimes seem such a puzzle to ourselves that we ask, 'Who am I?' We may even say of someone, 'He is not the person he was.' Of course, we cannot be anyone else, but in using such a phrase, we want to suggest something of the puzzle and contradiction that we find in ourselves. New ways of considering the contradictions and possibilities that are in us are always being explored. Today much work is being done on the central question of what it is to be a person at all – what do we mean by the 'real me'. These investigations are being conducted by secular philosophers and by Christian theologians and, despite real differences, there is a good deal of common ground.

This quest for the 'real me' has been stimulated by the marvellous work done in the fields of physics and biology. Recent discoveries have revolutionized our understanding of the interrelatedness of everything material. We can acknowledge that human beings too are made of matter, constituted of the same basic elements as everything else. From the skills of the geneticist and the microbiologist we can appreciate something of the way in which each human is unique, simply in the way that the 'code' that assembles the various components differs. There is cause for wonder at the way in which minute differences can result in people who are so infinitely varied. Further, the advances in understanding have made it clear that we can say a lot about the physical organism that is a human being, but there is still much to say about what makes that being a person – what makes me really me.

What, then, is the basis on which we build our understanding of being a human person? You see someone walking down the road and you say with confidence, 'There goes Alex'. Yet if you were to perform a thorough autopsy when Alex died (at any age) you would be unable to identify anything that could account for that very special and particular 'Alex-ness'. You could find evidence for some familiar characteristics, and evidence of those special skills and abilities you associate with Alex, yet something is missing. If Alex had been a great high-jumper, you would discover the muscle structure that brought success at the sport, but you could not find what gave inspiration and motivation for the necessary training and perseverance. What is more, it is not to be found anywhere else. The real Alex cannot be pinned down.

For generations we have spoken about a distinction between 'body' and 'soul'. Such a distinction has been used in various ways by philosophers and theologians with considerable care and refinement. In popular speech, however, there has been a widespread tendency to use the terms to suggest that the soul refers to the 'real person', to the essence of that man or woman, while the body refers to a kind of husk or container. Such use conflicts directly with a central part of Christian belief, for Christians proclaim in the creeds belief in 'the resurrection of the body'. But this too is not quite what it might seem at first sight. St Paul, to whom we owe most for our understanding of the way resurrection is worked out in us, is quite clear that death brings an end to our body of flesh. He speaks of the physical body being transformed at death, not into a soul suddenly set free, but into a spiritual body. In other words, Paul cannot accept a notion of the material body as a mere container. Rather, to be human, to be persons, we are necessarily embodied; we need a body. But death does indeed mean the end of our physical body as it has been, and so he speaks of our 'being raised a spiritual body'.

What makes us special?

This kind of difficulty has led some to suggest that we are in fact nothing more than the matter that forms us. We are material and nothing more, though we do not yet understand how some of the things that have no evident material aspect come to be: our thoughts and feelings, our personality and our psychological character. Others have pursued the opposite line and concluded that there is nothing material; everything is a mental state. The common sense rejection of both these approaches is clear, but confronts us again with the difficulty. Much recent writing has contributed fruitfully to a richer understanding of what it is to be a human person, but, from the Christian perspective, there is still some way to go. I know that I am more than a collection of cells, but it is still a puzzle to know how to speak of 'the real me'.

Theologians have pondered long and hard. Frequently they return to the beginning of Genesis where the writer speaks of humankind being made 'in the image and likeness of God'. Here is a rich and suggestive way of conveying something of what we mean by the 'Alex-ness' of Alex. Beyond the vast, intricate collection of cells that can be identified by scientific analysis there is in each of us the 'image and likeness of God'. Many attempts have been made to say just what this consists in. Much early theology identified the image with the capacity in humans for reason. Here, it was thought, was what marks human beings out from the rest of creation. This is the characteristic of God that is shared with humankind. God is the supreme principle of order and rationality and we are given a similar capacity for thinking and ordering. Yet the more we learn of the natural world, the more examples we see of complex rationality, order and interaction in things other than people. Some suggest that we can better describe this likeness to God in terms of human self-consciousness and self-awareness, but this has proved hard to pin down. Is it not more fruitful to consider what marks us out as persons? There are obvious advantages. Firstly, the word person has application to the whole woman or man. It does not have reference only to partial aspects of our being. Secondly, because it focuses on 'who' rather than 'what' we are, it helps us understand what we mean when we talk of 'fallen human nature' and 'redeemed humanity', of 'original creation' and 'original sin'.

The way through

One person holds the key to our quest for 'the real me'. At the heart of the gospel stands the person of Jesus Christ. In him questions about the world and the future *and* the search for ourselves are definitively answered. What it is to be a person receives a new shape and definition. Jesus Christ is unmistakably and wholly human and he is, at the same time, 'the image of the invisible God'. This revelation of God in our midst draws us towards the realization that Jesus Christ alone is truly a person. This immediately leads us to reflect on the way that we usually think of 'becoming a real person' as something that is the exclusive business of human beings. God may be some help and encouragement to us, but after all God is God, and this is something we have to get on with ourselves. In Jesus we see that this is not true. He fulfils everything we recognize as potential and which we desire in ourselves. And he does so, not by some kind of super-charged effort, but through the infinitely creative relationship he has with his 'Abba'. Such a relationship, per-fectly balanced and free from all competition, pours out into all his encounters – with his mother, his disciples, the sick and the hungry, and with those who follow him today. He is so completely himself, so complete in his identity, that those who heard him marvelled, for 'he taught with authority'.

We know well that there are difficulties in saying anything of God for we run the risk of making God in our own image, or, in another way, making him less than God. Yet, as Michael Ramsey taught, 'in God there is no un-Christlikeness', and so we may speak from our knowledge of Jesus Christ. We do not say of him with admiration, 'He was a *real* person' as though he had somehow done well to achieve what belongs to us. Rather we say that he is the only real and complete person there is. Because Jesus Christ is 'the only Son of the Father' what is true of him is true of God. The Father is made visible in the person of the Son and in recognizing the Son as the source of life we are drawn towards the God who is Father, Son and Holy Spirit, and is the source and giver of all.

The nature of the gift

Becoming truly and fully a person – finding the 'real me' – now appears not as something we can work at, like becoming a good gardener or a good highjumper. Rather, our knowledge of Jesus Christ tells us that it is something we receive, it is a gift. This gift of God is offered to us in two characteristic ways which are not alternatives, but equally necessary and correspond to the great commandment in the synoptic Gospels, 'You shall love the Lord your God with all your heart, and with all your soul, and with all your strength, and with all your mind; and your neighbour as yourself' (Luke 10.27).

Firstly, in our living and caring for each other we are constantly giving and exchanging or withholding and refusing something of that 'image and likeness' of God which marks us all. There is a marked contrast between a baby born of love into a loving family and a child conceived without love. Such a child, brought into the world by a mother who has taken no thought for the unborn child during pregnancy, and without the support of the natural father, emerges at birth as a tiny human form, physically normal but deprived of love and care. Such withholding of the gift is a mark of sin in us – and now it is the sin which is passed on: in this tiny human being we see the absence of love and care before birth and a disadvantaged beginning to life in

12

the world. For such a baby, becoming a person is a much greater struggle than for one conceived in love and loved into life.

Secondly, there is the new life in Christ to which baptism is the gateway. Here, too, we receive the gifts of love and care. Just as Jesus once walked among us, revealing the marvellous potential in humankind through the giftedness of his being with the Father and the Spirit, drawing riches out of others through his gifts of healing and teaching, so now we are enabled by his grace at work in us to receive the gift of ourselves at the Father's hands. It is true that we receive much that makes us real from all those whose lives are linked with ours, but the one who alone can make us complete is God, our Creator and Redeemer. This way of mutual exchange is necessarily true of creation, but a new dimension of it is revealed in our glad response to the call of Christ. Baptism into Christ is the acknowledgement of our need which brings us into life in the Church where we receive the gifts of the Spirit. We are drawn into fellowship with one another and find ourselves at home within a greater fellowship, *koinonia* – the Trinity.

At first sight, the debates and complex doctrinal formulations of the Church seem to have little to do with the questions that actually trouble and preoccupy us. Eager theological debate about the Trinity is hardly what you expect to hear in the local pub. Yet the New Testament, though we often overlook this, vibrates with urgency and excitement as it tells of men and women wrestling with new and demanding possibilities. It is a kaleidoscopic account, given by people who know what they are talking about, of something they describe as 'salvation'. This salvation is something that they have received, and by which they have been transformed. It does not appear out of thin air; it is not something they have stumbled upon after long hours of research; it is not a technique they have learned: it is a gift. The giver is Jesus Christ. And this Jesus Christ is utterly human and utterly God. Nothing short of a unique kind of loving and being together can account for this revolution in our understanding of who God is, and what it is to be a person. It was to try to grasp something of this that the early Christians dared to speak of the Father and the Son as being 'of one substance'.

When Paul, writing to the Corinthians, says, 'For as in Adam all die, so also in Christ shall all be made alive' (1 Cor. 15.22), he is putting into words something of his own experience. From

13

time to time you feel a frustration in him as the language at his disposal appears too rough hewn and imprecise for what he is struggling to say. Nonetheless we can hear what he is saying. We know something of what he means. Central to his vision is the realization that in Jesus Christ, crucified, buried and raised to new life, we are confronted with what being a person is all about. Here is something new. Here is identity and meaning, seen in Jesus Christ and offered to us through him. We might have thought we understood before but we were mistaken. When my sister used to say to her one year old daughter, 'Hallo, small person,' there was obvious humour in the remark. An infant *is* a small person, complete in all essentials. Yet we are most aware of potential, not of a finished person. Jesus Christ is the one who was unmistakably 'real' and through him we too may become truly ourselves.

Persons and parsons

Being a creature

We are finally and helplessly dependent. Dependent on each other and, supremely, dependent on God. That is what it means to be a creature. The knowledge and acceptance of this can seem frustrating and an admission of defeat. Awareness of God brings with it awareness of sin. 'Sin' is, contrary to much popular use, a theological term. Its essential meaning has to do with the relation between God and the creation. God made, God saw, and it was good. Our experience, on the other hand, is of things being sometimes good, but often failing to live up to their promise, and sometimes of things being bad in a way that defies explanation or resolution. And what we observe around us is true of ourselves too. We certainly sin repeatedly and it is right to speak of actions, thoughts and words as sinful. Yet more profoundly we have to recognize that we *are* sin. We shall not easily accept St Augustine's phrase 'a lump of sin' as the best description of ourselves, but facile statements about the essential goodness of human beings will not do either. In a way that we would not wish, and in a way that we can do nothing about, we are thoroughly caught up in sin in a way that forces us to recognize that it is not simply something external to us. Original sin is sometimes made to seem like a nasty hereditary disease that we cannot avoid and which is always fatal, but for the grace of God. This too has the weakness of viewing sin as something that has invaded from outside and has the disadvantage of encouraging us to irresponsibility and blaming someone else for our predicament. In trying to speak of the way in which God in Christ comes to meet us in our need St Paul says, 'For our sake he made him to be sin who knew no sin, so that in him we might become the righteousness of God' (2 Cor. 5.21). At the heart of original sin is a striving for independence from the Creator that is essentially pre-conscious in the face of a necessary dependence.

Dependence transformed

The cross of Christ is the means and the dramatic symbol of our liberation from helplessness and futility. Through commitment to Christ in baptism and to one another in the communion of faith, acceptance of our need of God may become the receiving of the gift which transforms dependence into the way of life. In him, through him and with him we 'are to grow up in every way into him who is the head, into Christ' (Eph. 4.15). We, who have some awareness of the gift we receive through our baptism into Christ, are to help bring others to know what it is to become 'real', to help them grow into true personhood. All that we desire we see fulfilled in Christ and so we gladly acknowledge that God is the source of all that we mean by the word 'person' and find joy in our dependence on him.

Our present preoccupation with what it means to be a person is largely Western and expresses the dominant form of our current attempt to achieve autonomy. This preoccupation may lead us further from God or it may bring us to that change of heart that the New Testament calls *metanoia*, conversion. Susan Hill, in her novel *Strange Meeting*, gives a powerful parable of conversion in her account of the relationship between two soldiers in the Great War. Barton believes in Hilliard – in his goodness, his capacities, his gifts – and Hilliard, as a result of this unselfconscious, generous being-believed-in, is quite simply converted in the sense that he becomes a new person.

The Christian is one who has chosen to accept the invitation of God, to walk with Christ Jesus. To enter into new life with

Christ is to find encouragement for the frail echoes of person-hood we already know. It is to discover at an inexpressible depth the faithfulness of God which gives us a true faith in ourselves. It is also to be drawn towards new possibilities that are opened to us as we accept the gospel path. The dramatic images of the New Testament speak powerfully of the nature of the journey that must be made: 'For the Son of man also came not to be served, but to serve . . .' (Mark 10.45); 'as dying, and behold we live' (2 Cor. 6.9); 'For whoever would save his life will lose it, and whoever loses his life for my sake will find it' (Matt. 16.25). Such challenges are empty without the living example of the one who was betrayed and given into the hands of the wicked, was crucified, died and was buried. Empty too without the hitherto unimaginable response of God 'who raised him from the dead that our faith and hope might be in God'.

Universal and particular

In Susan Hill's novel there is a powerful contrast between the vast, appalling events of the war and the intimate exchange between the two soldiers; on the one hand the universal and the general with all its horror, and on the other the particular and the apparently insignificant, which radiates love and goodness. This contrast again takes us to the heart of the gospel. The distortions of this world which we describe as sin and evil are everywhere. Their horrors are only too familiar to us. The incarnation of Jesus Christ was the necessary response of the love of God. The mystery of love loving us into life had to be particularized. The Saviour had to be the one who was lost, betrayed and killed, in order that we might believe. The offer had to be created and made in our midst, not because of some weakness in God, but because of our sin and frailty.

God's response to our sin and frailty was the gift of his Son, who took our nature and lived among us. Our frailty today is one with those to whom Jesus preached and those whom he healed. The need for the offer of salvation to be particularized among us remains. In the mercy of God, the Church exists as the body of Christ. It is the company of those who have recognized the fullness of being in Jesus Christ and seek to follow him. In the generosity of God, this gathering of human persons is no mere society, but a real representation of the life of Christ.

Room for the parson

Within this fellowship are those who, called by God and the Church and set apart by ordination, live out their conviction and belief that Christ is the one true person. The priestly life is public and it is sacramental. It is another particularizing, as both encouragement and witness. In specific acts of service it may rightly be said that effectiveness and validity do not depend on the worthiness or faith of the priest. The heart of the priest's ministry is the making visible of the gift of personhood which is Christ's alone. It is no accident that the parish priest in England became known as the parson, the *persona* who represents Christ to his people. Such representation demands an integrity of faith and life that both points to Christ and reveals the fruitfulness of faith in Christ. It demands that the priest be one who has an evident confidence in Christ as the giver of the self.

Much of our human experience is of disappointment and failure. We long to 'be someone' yet our hopes seem unattainable. In response, the Christian tradition reveals to us the God who creates and redeems. What seemed futile and empty is set before us afresh in terms of offer and gift. George Herbert, in a poem called simply 'Priesthood', takes two powerful and ancient images. He speaks of us as clay, and God, the maker and redeemer, as fire. At once we see the distance from God that talk about sin indicates and we sense the power of God to overcome the gap. Jesus Christ is the giver of God; and the Christian priest, through a life of faith in the giver and service to the Church which is his body, is called to be a gift to the world – to open the eyes of the blind and bring liberty to captives – so that the clay of the world may be transformed by the fire of God. If we are to appreciate the distinctiveness of the priest's calling we must give our attention next to the shape of the Church, for only within and as a part of the Church does any talk of a priest make sense.

CHAPTER TWO

How do we belong?

'Your plants look half dead,' said Mr Hill. 'You need to water
them properly and give them a good feed.'

Alison hadn't noticed them for some time, life had been so
busy. They stood there on the windowsill looking as if life was a
struggle to survive, many of their leaves dried up and brown at
the edges.

'Yes,' she sighed, 'yet another demand on my time. Excuse
me, Mr Hill, I've got to go and see the Fords.'

He carried on trying to fix the gas stove – they were lucky to
have such a helpful neighbour.

'A real tragedy,' he said as she went. 'Motor bikes should be
banned.'

The Fords were in a daze, still far from taking in the fact that
they had lost their eldest son. The visit from the curate was very
much appreciated – they all prayed together before she went.
Brian was looking after them too – it was only right that the
vicar do that for a family who were pillars of the parish. Alison
was closely involved because of the youth club. She went away
ill at ease. We have said a prayer, she thought, but what else
have I done that couldn't have been done by a friendly social
worker? Is the Church just a decoration for all of us? The night
before the funeral the coffin was brought into church and family

and friends came to a Eucharist. That was obviously very powerful for them.

Mr Hill was back on the day of the funeral with a replacement spare part, and Alison voiced some of her uncertainties – he was an understanding man, and easy to talk to.

'I remember when Margery died,' he reflected. 'I thought then that the vicar didn't talk about God when he came. But he talks about God enough from the pulpit. Then I thought about those clergy who do talk about God – you know the sort – and I remember thinking, 'Thank God I didn't get one of them'. Clergy are only human. For all of us faith is frail, and such occasions must make a priest very aware of his own inadequacy. I don't blame them for that. God is a two-way matter. Perhaps there's something wrong with all of us that makes God unmentionable,' and he looked up at the plants again, which were still wilting. 'The most important thing, you know, was that the vicar had been. It was as if you knew God had recognized us and put Margery's death on the map. Those are moments when the Church can seem strong stuff, you know.'

Alison was married to a Romanian. Peter's father had just died, and they went over together. They came to one of those dreary areas of concrete blocks put up by the communists. Peter's father was laid out on the bed, surrounded by family and neighbours, each holding a lighted candle with a circle of bread around it. A priest in vestments was singing and swinging his thurible, the people joining in. That typified the whole affair, complicated and exhausting. Alison realized of course that here was a priest talking about God, but in a way that was both bearable and capable of endless spinning-out. They don't expect him to say what can only be said in poetry if at all. Only poetry is worthy of death. She found herself rather surprised to find this penny dropping. Here the Church was powerful and real.

'I don't know how you Westerners cope,' said Peter, fastening the safety belt for the flight back. 'You seem to rely on comforting people with platitudes.'

'That's not fair,' Alison said. 'What do you know about it?'

'You only have to look,' he said. 'Your religion is invisible. You have everything that we've got, but it's all watered down and thin.'

Surprisingly enough, Peter found no difficulty in being married to a deacon. He understood what it was about and respected it, even though a female diaconate was far from Orthodox practice.

'I grant you,' said Alison, 'that there is a lot you can teach us, but our cultures are so different. The British aren't religious by nature, and we are reserved, while you Romanians are demonstrative and romantic. I'm always amazed, Peter, at how well you fit in.'

'We are perfectly complementary,' he beamed, as he put his arm around her. 'You and I are an inter-cultural project. That is what Romania is. And our church, like yours, needs many reforms, but at least it is strong wine. That is what Christ meant his Church to be.'

They found Mr Hill still struggling with the cooker. He was in the oven and Alison needed the grill. They were starving.

'You know,' she said, as she leaned over him to stab the window ajar with a breadknife, 'the Church is in need of a revolution.'

'I'm sure it is,' came a voice from inside the oven, 'but if you'll let me say so, your plants are still waiting for one, too.'

The Christian who asks, 'Who is the real me?' cannot avoid referring to the New Testament. When we look there for information about our identity, one thing that strikes us is the frequent reference to community. Jesus laid great emphasis on the unity of his followers; in John's Gospel we are given the image of the vine and the branches; Paul on the other hand speaks of our being the body of Christ, in which each person has individual gifts and roles and in this way is like an organ in the totality of the human body. This theme is fundamental to the New Testament vision of what it means to be 'me'.

Terms which commonly recur in the New Testament are 'Body' and 'Church' (*ekklesia*). The word 'Church' has gained, with the passage of time, both positive and negative associations. Many Christians seem allergic to the term, perceiving it to suggest hierarchies, legal structures, and tightly-defined institutions that seem far from the character of Jesus of Nazareth. These problems, however, have cropped up right from the beginning. We only have to witness James and John asking for privileged places in the kingdom, or the misdoings of the church at Corinth, to recognize that there is a powerful tendency to reduce the Church to the merely human level. If Christ founded a community, then it was inevitable that it should have structures and roles (and so Peter emerges as a leader, John as a charismatic figure, Judas as the keeper of the common purse, and so on). If the structures are inevitable, and are open to misuse, how may we use them well? How can the body of Christ be something which is faithful to Christ without distorting him or us?

Structures

Human societies usually require leadership, administration, allotting of tasks, and so on. Whether they be tribes, darts clubs or nations, such structures naturally emerge within them. At one level they fulfil necessary *functions*: administration needs to be co-ordinated, children to be taught, roads to be mended; but roles in society operate on several further planes. For one thing, they have an effect on the *character* of the persons who fulfil them. This can sometimes be so marked that the jobs people do can be guessed from their bearing and behaviour. It may be obvious when someone is a soldier, a market trader, or teacher. The role can also take on a life of its own: it can exert such a hold that the person's whole life is *identified* with it, perhaps to the degree of obsession. For example, there is the businessman who lives for nothing but takeover bids, the politician consumed by politics, the athlete thinking of nothing but the next contest. Then another layer still is that of *value*: we might pull the leg of our next-door neighbour but not do so with the doctor. There are appropriate degrees of familiarity or deference. This can easily be corrupted by its recipient into a matter of status. This has been the bugbear of structures in society throughout human history. At times, furthermore, roles can gain metaphysical or *symbolic* significance. A king or queen symbolizes the nation in a way which could be called spiritual; a football team can symbolize a whole world of hopes and fears for its fans. Structure in society works in all these ways, and more besides.

It seems to be the case that human society naturally evolves such structures. It may be true that their particular character has tended to be determined by dominantly patriarchal traits in society, traits which are now being challenged. It is difficult to see, however, how complex societies can function without leadership of some kind and without allocation of responsibilities. The fact that such roles stand in need of transformation goes without saying, and Christ's gospel aims precisely at revolutionizing structures of relationship. Any society, and that includes the Church, will need (and so will evolve) structures, and similarities between those in the Church and those in other forms of society can be drawn. But in the Church it has been different from the start, because of the relation of roles to the person of Christ. This still holds true even though this difference has at times been badly eroded. Christians can slip into seeing church structures in the same terms as those of the secular world. In the Middle Ages, for instance, roles came to be distorted by the feudal mentality, and what should have expressed humility and service turned more and more into hierarchies of power. We see perhaps the same thing happening today, as Christians look too indiscriminately to such contemporary role models as the therapist and the manager. Professional models, and even the attitudes and style of society, need much closer vetting before passing into Christian usage. This should not lead us into a mistrust of the notion of role itself: distinctive roles are inevitable in human society, and problems sometimes experienced in the Church arise from an interpretation of them which has fallen under the influence of the contemporary world, rather than the figure of Christ.

The Church develops its texture

It was already decided amongst the fishing-nets of Galilee that Christ's followers were not to be a shapeless crowd but should fall into some kind of formation. Some were called to leave everything and follow him. They were to give themselves as completely as possible to accompanying Christ closely and directly. These were the 'twelve'. Among them several, such as Peter and John, had a particular place. Then there were others, the larger body of disciples. Among these too there were various ones whose role was distinctive, such as the several Marys. All the time Jesus was insistent that such things were matters of relationship, not power, and of role, not status. In order to make the point clear he turned the structures topsy-turvy: all who were at the 'top' were at the bottom; all who might be thought to be at the 'bottom' were at the top. The topsy-turviness was redoubled by the reflection that those who thought they were at the bottom but were at the top should also realize that the 'top' involved the cross.

In the New Testament writings we see the future orders of the Church beginning to emerge: bishops, presbyters (from which we get the English word 'priest')and deacons are all mentioned, but as yet there is little clear definition of their distinctiveness. 'Bishop' and 'presbyter' seem to be interchangeable, and the *diakonia* (a word with many resonances associated with the notion of 'service') which characterizes the deacon's role also characterizes the other two. There are other roles too, house-holder (Chloe et al.), speaker in tongues, interpreter, and so forth. Prophets at that period were very important, for they seem sometimes to have presided at the Eucharist. The word 'preface' seems to derive from the word 'prophecy', a word which was originally used to designate the whole eucharistic prayer. We cannot at this period speak of 'clergy', a term which arose in the Middle Ages. There is simply a multiplicity of roles, implied in the gifts listed by St Paul, a kaleidoscope as varied as the kinds of people who made it up.

Early on it came to be thought that bishops, presbyters and deacons had to be ordained by the laying on of hands. There are signs of this already in the New Testament, but as with most other aspects of the primitive Church, contemporary documents reveal to us a vortex of variety: order was only gradually established, as Christians worked out the consequences of realizing they were the Body of Christ. Some early documents reveal that for a time confessors were automatically treated as priests even though they did not receive the laying on of hands, for God had clearly laid hands on them in their sufferings. Eventually, however, hand-laying became obligatory. By the fourth century at the very latest the traditional understanding of the threefold ministry and apostolic succession had become established. The guarantors of this were seen to be various things: faithfulness to the apostolic tradition, as it evolved out of the New Testament in the succeeding centuries by the general consensus of the Church; the foundation of Christian communities from 'apostolic' churches in a chain which can be traced back to the apostles themselves (i.e. founded by missionaries, not by reading a book, or setting up 'freelance'); the faithfulness of each particular community in its living out of the gospel within the apostolic tradition; and a 'tactile' succession of the ordained ministry through episcopal laying on of hands.

Western doctrine on the Church came to lay particular stress on the last element, through the influence of Roman law and increasing preoccupation with the 'validity' of sacraments (this is not to imply that it is not of great importance in the East). While the tactile succession is extremely primitive in its origins, we now know that it does not become a universal prerequisite until after the time of the apostles themselves. Some very careful work still remains to be done to identify the effective content of this primitive tradition. The 'bridge' between the apostolic age and the establishment of universally accepted order in the Church can be compared to a prism. In the apostolic period the whole gospel mystery was, as it were, a bright, white light, a diffuse and totally encompassing experience, with little differentiation of its constituent elements. This could not continue – it had to pass through the prism of sorting-and-ordering to emerge separated out in the various colours of doctrine, orders, sacraments, and so on. This does not give us the freedom to see the tactile succession as optional. If we decide to dismantle one of these elements, then we must recognize we are dismantling the whole spectrum, and will need to start all over again with the unique bright light of the apostolic experience. There is, however, no going back, as all attempts to reproduce the New Testament Church have shown. We are no more free, on the other hand, to build more on the tactile succession than its gradual evolution allows. The apostolic succession has always to be considered in the integral context of the 'economy' of the Church, in whichever period it is examined. Benedict Green points out that the New Testament canon and the apostolic ministry of bishops, presbyters and deacons emerge together and for much the same reason. We 'cannot now easily assent to the literal sense of the statement of the Preface of the Ordinal [of the BCP] that "from the Apostles' time there have been these orders of ministers in Christ's Church, bishops, priests and deacons," nor say with the full support of the historian that the monarchical bishops who made their appearance in the second century could trace their episcopal authority back through a continuous succession of laying-on of hands to the original apostles; but we can claim that ... this was the providence of

God. As Dr Austin Farrer has summed it up: "The apostolic testimony was a divine gift; it settled into the scriptures of the new covenant, and we have canonised the scriptures. The apostolic ministry was likewise a divine gift; it settled into the episcopate, and we have canonised the office." [1]

Here we need to return to Jesus himself. In him people met with an extraordinary manifestation of the divine. He was unique. That which was in Christ distinguished him from all other people, and extraordinary effects flowed from it. Jesus initiated something, and this was to continue until he came again. So in the early Church we see a sovereign outpouring of the Spirit in a kaleidoscope of gifts of extraordinary vitality. As it came more and more to be seen that Christ was not to return immediately, questions began to be asked. Where can we identify the work of the Spirit? How can this unleashing of power not be dissipated in an organization growing larger and larger, and ever more widely spread? How can it all be held together and not split up? They started in effect to 'map' areas where they could be reasonably sure of what was what. They were not at first certain how the gift for presiding at the Eucharist could be identified, but their deductions led them to conclude that it could definitely be 'mapped' at least among bishops and presbyters. So in a similar manner the other external structures of the Church came to be established. It was by a process of identification rather than prescription. In other words, although it was recognized that the Spirit moves where he wills, and the manifestation of gifts of God in the Church was unpredictable, it was nevertheless possible to identify areas where some things could be nailed down, and, if the body of Christ was to be faithful to its calling, this needed to be done. The end result was a body of Christ which had gained more of the characteristics of a human institution. The institutional side included the larger mystery but did not exhaust it. Thenceforward it often threatened to shrink down to the proportions of a *mere* institution, and frequently needed to be recalled to the fact that what it 'mapped' may be precise, but this was for urgent practical purposes, and should not obscure the fact that true edges were blurred, and beyond the map lay further dimensions of the same reality.

Ecumenism

One of our problems in a divided Church is that different parts of the Church have come up with different maps. We are dependent on our maps, and uncertain about straying from them, and hence the problems that ecumenism faces today. The failure of negotiation at the 'top' has led to action lower down, at more informal levels, much of which is helping the churches to grow together. It ranges from ecumenical co-operation in the fields of social service or study to the establishment of ecumenical parishes. There are many areas where much more can be done together but is not being done, such as marriage preparation, or addressing with a public voice the state of society, or weekday worship and daily office, or the life of religious communities. A very long list could be compiled.

This problem has a direct bearing on what we are saying about priesthood. There seems to be a need both for much greater ecumenical involvement and on a much larger scale than is the case at the moment, but also a need for some fine tuning in areas where we may be being trigger-happy because what is at stake is more invisible than visible. First of all, those churches which have a threefold ministry can not easily sidestep it, and yet this should in no way prevent us seeking to understand and give due respect to each others' ministries wihout an easy cutting of corners which leaves no one living out of a rooted tradition. What we do not want is a superficial amalgam now which fails to respect the differences and historic tensions that we inherit and which to some extent still determine our attitudes.

Secondly, picking and choosing from a range of ecumenical sweets does not serve integrity – we should be careful that all the churches are involved in balance as far as is humanly (and divinely) possible. Otherwise we are fated to end up with two or three opposed blocks in place of a more versatile melange in process of convergence.

Thirdly, ecumenism cannot escape the past. Mark Santer, in an illuminating article, reminds us that 'it is by the things we fail to remember, that we identify ourselves as belonging to [a] group'.[2] In any serious ecumenical endeavour the past has to be faced sooner of later. Present differences are the front for all manner of tacit assumptions of whose existence we are scarcely aware. Ecumenism is a process that is at once spiritual, intellectual and ascetic, recollecting in humility both what is good and what has hurt others in the corporate memory. If it is to be more than mere collaboration, it calls for the same qualities that make for holiness and the readiness for a new knowledge of self and of others, conversion in fact. As the Roman Catholic Second Vatican Council so memorably put it: 'This change of heart and holiness of life ... should be regarded as the soul of the whole ecumenical movement, and merits the name "spiritual ecumenism".'[3] This means that a deep immersion in the tradition of our particular communion, its life, common worship and spirituality, becomes not an obstacle to ecumenical work, but a prerequisite. We have argued that the distinctive gift of priesthood is one shaped and formed by the whole life of God's priestly people. It is neither possible nor desirable therefore to iron out, or put in parentheses, different ministerial structures with their different 'memories', without distorting the gift God has given.

A gingerly approach is required, with sufficient imagination to venture beyond our apparent certainties and, with occasional inspired breaking of the rules, to work for that unity which must surely be God's will for his Church, while at the same time not wantonly devaluing and selling off things of importance in a kind of back-door ecumenism without tears. Involvement of selected other churches in decision-making over the running of ordination training in the Church of England is a glaring example of such selectivity which may easily result in strained ecumenical relationships.

Repeatedly there has been the tendency to see the 'map' as defining the whole reality, rather than just that part that seems clear to us. This falling away and recovery is perpetual, like Peter's intermittently successful walking on the water. As often as we treat the Church as a human institution, we are falling back in effect to the position before the incarnation, either through a return to the Law (e.g. some aspects of the medieval Church), or through playing down of the physical Church as a manifestation of the incarnation (e.g. modern criticism of 'churchiness'). It is a natural pastime of humanity to undo the incarnation, and never more so than in the twentieth century. Particularly today there are many who incline to a view that ordained ministry shows all the characteristics of roles in society (including their tendency to corruption) and nothing more. This, however, is almost impossible to reconcile with the vision of the body of Christ presented to us in the New Testament. There we see that the body is more than just a human organization like any other: it is in effect *sacrament*. In order to explain this we need to recapitulate a little.

God's presence in his creation

'And God saw everything that he had made, and behold, it was very good' (Gen. 1.31). Then came the Fall: but despite the imperfection portrayed in the story of the Fall, Christianity sees creation to be good, and to contain within itself something of the image of its maker. So it dares to proclaim his incarnation within the very world he had made. Our God is discernible in his creation. The cosmos is like a book in which we read of him who is its creator, and so are aided on our journey towards him. 'The heavens are telling the glory of God, and the firmament proclaims his handiwork' (Ps. 19.1). However, because of the tension between good and evil, all we can receive are intimations of him, and he remains distant and inscrutable, despite the growing reassurance people gain of his faithful loving kindness. This was the situation of the Jews at the time of Jesus. The world was known to be holy; and so were daily life, human work and enjoyment, friendship and family life, and the community and the nation: the holiness of these things was sensed. And yet there was a hint of something more: for people came to say that creation is not only a book which tells us about God, but it actually mediates him, puts him and us in touch with one another. They found God, after all, in a burning bush, in a pillar of fire, in the Law, and in the Temple.

Not only that, but they could see he was active in all the ordinary things of life:

> All of them look to you to give them their food in due season; you give it to them, they gather it; you open your hand and they are filled with good things. (Ps. 104.28f)

And there is still more, for he is the very mystery of life itself which is within us:

> You take away their breath and they die. ... You
> send forth your Spirit and they are created. (Ps.
> 104.30f)

God is in the midst of his creation, and is to be known
through it. This presence of God is especially true in humanity,
so much so that for the author of Genesis human persons are
made in God's 'image' (Gen. 1.26). These things went quite a
long way to identifying the presence of God in his physical
creation, but they were still not enough. For there remained a
paradox which seemed unresolvable: God was both very close
and yet at the same time hopelessly distant, 'other'. He was like
us, so that it might seem that we might be united with him as
music is married to words in a song. However, at the same time
the gulf between us and him remained so utter that to bridge it
would be as impossible as uniting rust with love, or grammar
with cheese. Such a gulf could never be bridged. Or so we
thought. The New Testament thinks otherwise: it claims that
the seemingly impossible thing actually happened with the birth
of Christ. In this audacious turn of events our perception of the
presence of God in the world was to be revolutionized.

Perfected in Christ

In Christ our ability to relate to God in creation is released from
its blockage and set on the road away from imperfection
towards perfection. In Christ himself we see it already perfected:
he is fully God and fully man. In him those who believed saw
something new: no longer an intimation of God's presence in
creation, but that very presence itself. His humanity joined with
ours, uniting us to him like a song's words to its music; but, and
this is the dramatic change, it also opened the way to our unity
with God, as if cheese and grammar were indeed now to merge.
In Christ the impossible bridging takes place: we see a limited
human being, but one in whom the presence of God is now
manifest, not merely intimated. The fire and the clay have
become one. With him is ushered in a new way of relating to
God: the *sacramental* order of the body of Christ. Before we can
discuss this further, we need to look a little more closely at the
meaning of the word 'sacrament'.

Sacraments

Sacraments are physical things and actions, usually accompanied by particular forms of words, which put us in touch with God in a unique way. The uniqueness is partly that they are not just symbols but bring about that which they express. So in baptism the water, together with the words, 'I baptize you in the name of the Father, and of the Son, and of the Holy Spirit', illustrate powerfully the dramatic change which God brings about in those who turn to Christ. However, not only does it illustrate – something happens in it which happens in no other pourings of water. God does something to us through this water. It is the same with the Eucharist and with the other sacraments. A physical action with bread and wine and the use of certain words becomes a sign which effects that which it signifies. When described like this, sacraments may seem like magic, but the point which is more difficult to explain in simple terms is that we are not speaking here of the conveying of some 'power', like an electric current, nor about something like the waving of a magic wand.

The root of it lies in the word 'mystery', which occurs many times in the New Testament. The Greek *mysterion* is often unfortunately translated by such words as 'secret', but if we look up 'mysterion' in a Greek concordance we shall be surprised at the number of times it appears in the New Testament. Its commonest use is to refer to the mystery of Christ, his incarnation, death and resurrection, and his exaltation in glory. All of this is the mystery, 'hidden for ages and generations but now made manifest to his saints. To them God chose to make known how great among the gentiles are the riches of the glory of this mystery, which is Christ in you, the hope of glory' (Col. 1.26f). When the word 'mysterion' was translated in the West, we Westerners for various reason came to prefer the word 'sacrament' as a translation of it. When therefore we speak of the sacraments, we are speaking not of magical actions, but of this mystery of Christ. The sacraments are the 'mysteries', gifts to us from God in which we meet the mystery of Christ. In baptism we enter into the mystery of his death and resurrection. 'Do you not know that all of us who have been baptized into Christ Jesus were baptized into his death? We were buried therefore with him by baptism into death, so that as Christ was raised from the dead by the glory of the Father, we too might walk in newness of life' (Rom. 6.3f). In the Eucharist, the 'holy mysteries' as the Book of Common Prayer calls them (and for this reason), we receive in the bread and wine not some special power from God, but rather the presence of Christ incarnate, crucified and risen. We enter through a door into the 'mystery which was hidden for long ages' but is now revealed (Rom. 16.25). The 'something' which happens in the sacraments is the mystery of Christ. It happens to us in visible form and invisible form. What we can see is the water, or the bread and wine, or the laying on of hands, and so on. What we cannot see with our physical eyes are the nativity, cross, resurrection and all the other saving events which envelop us in the sacraments, and transform us. We are in fact seeing them, but in the form of water, or bread and wine, or the other visible forms of the sacraments.

Our modern way of life does not mesh well with the Christian notion of the sacraments. We are practical, utilitarian, sceptical. For us everything needs to be objectively tested and verified. We might be superstitious about the number thirteen, or credulous about the healing properties of neolithic stone circles, but, apart from such minor breaking of the rules, we remain in most senses 'down to earth' in our outlook on life. We therefore need a good deal of persuading when it comes to the sacramental theology of tradition. For this says that physical acts such as baptism and the Eucharist belong to the new order ushered in by Christ: they participate in the uniqueness of the incarnation. So they bring together things which we are convinced are incommensurate: our humanity with God's divinity, closely associated with a little piece of created matter, in simple human actions. By the water in baptism something is effected which no other water can do; the bread in the Eucharist unites us with God in such a way that it is totally different from the ordinary bread it was a few minutes ago.

That is a simplified outline of what is implied by sacramentality: it carries forward what the incarnation began. Within this simple outline certain other things become clear. First of all, the sacraments do not operate automatically. Just as Christ allowed the rich young man to go away, so also the sacraments depend on engaging with an interior response. But such a response cannot be evaluated easily by us; our responses to God are always inadequate, and depth psychology has taught us that there is much more at work in us than the merely conscious mind. I may be absent-minded in my response to a person, a symphony, or Holy Communion, and yet be responding at an unconscious level of my mind's onion-layers. This is why we are never in a position to judge whether a response to a sacrament has been adequate – only God can judge. This is also why we also have to be extremely cautious about speaking of 'worthy' reception of the sacraments. We are never worthy, but God out of his graciousness is always prepared to receive us. This is also why the Thirty Nine Articles state that the effectiveness of the sacraments does not depend on the worthiness of the minister. The sacraments do not operate automatically, but neither does their fruitfulness depend only on the person's 'state of mind'. God alone is sovereign here, and only he knows how he is working among people.

Secondly, the sacraments cannot simply be spoken of as dispensing grace: they are more precise than that. They are directly connected with the birth, life, death and resurrection of Jesus. They involve us spiritually and physically in particular aspects of these salvation events: we encounter these events and engage with them. By the later Middle Ages sacramental theology had tended to see the sacraments as providing dollops of grace, a substance measured out, as it were, by the yard. The connection with the saving events of Christ had become obscured, and so sacraments could be understood as dispensing something like a magical power. St Paul gives us a different picture, according to which the sacraments connect us up with Christ himself, and nothing less, and it is the Christ of the New Testament: in baptism we are buried with Christ and rise again with him (burial and resurrection); in the Eucharist we show forth his death, until he comes again (death and second coming). This is not just power or shapeless grace, but Christ the grace-filled one incorporating us into the saving events. It is by those deeds that we are saved, and it is in them that we are deluged with God's grace. According to Leo the Great, 'What was visible in the Lord has passed into the sacraments.' The sacraments are a consequence of the incarnation. The dynamite at the heart of them is the resurrection. The sacraments insert us into the saving narrative, so that we live it, and become, as it were, Christs. This can come home to us at Christmas, or in the Holy Week liturgy, or when we are anointed in sickness, or when we hear the assurance of forgiveness in the words of the Body of Christ. What is quite clear is that we are not simply dealing with quantities of something powerful: we are experiencing an encounter with, and involvement in, all of that which is described in the Gospels. This very primitive sketch now allows us to examine how we may talk of Christ as 'sacrament'.

Christ the sacrament

Just as the sacraments can be seen to work on the principle of the incarnation, so conversely it is often said that the incarnate Christ is the primary sacrament. The old intimation of God's presence in creation is fulfilled in a new opening of the door between two worlds in Christ the sacrament. What was formerly shadowed forth is now reality: '... the Law has but a shadow of the good things to come instead of the true form of these realities ... [but] we have confidence to enter the sanctuary by the blood of Jesus, by the new and living way which he opened for us through the curtain, that is, through his flesh ...' (Heb. 10.1, 19f). The reason we can say that Jesus is the fundamental sacrament without being confused is found in the word 'mystery' which we have already met. The glorious mystery now revealed which is referred to in the New Testament is Christ himself, and what the sacraments do is put us in touch with that New Testament mystery. As we have seen, the words 'sacrament' and 'mystery' are really the same thing.

Christ has taken all that is good in what it is to be human and brought it together in a new synthesis with the divine. All those who are taken up into the sacrament of Christ's body the Church are affected by this, and its typically human structures have this added dimension. A bishop, a priest, a deacon, a reader, a server, a musician, a flower arranger, fulfil roles which can be paralleled in ordinary human society but (whether good examples of it or not) they act out in their roles the mystery of the incarnation; they make present the sacrament of the Church. They are a presence of Jesus. They are clay inhabited by fire.

The Church carries it on

It took some time for the early Church to realize the full implications of this. In the oldest parts of the New Testament such as the letters of Paul or the synoptic Gospels it was perceived in a very undifferentiated way, inchoate and unsorted. There was a perception of the unique 'belongingness' of the baptized, and that this was so sacramental (to use a later terminology) that God in Christ was vitally present in them and thereby available to the world. Put simply, they themselves were Christ the sacrament. (In fact the New Testament does use the word 'sacrament' like this, through the word 'mystery'.) They were his body – his uniqueness was in them. Only gradually did this truth come to be articulated and analysed more closely, and in that process distinctive shapes emerged, especially the Scriptures, church structures, forms of worship and sacraments, and the incipient working out of doctrine.

In all this process of sorting, the limitation of sacraments to seven or to two came very late on: in the patristic period people could see sacraments all over the place. There is a great need to move beyond the unnatural limitations of the medieval seven and rediscover the manifold nature of the sacraments. This was to some extent acknowledged in designating a secondary order of practices as 'sacramentals', but all of this misses the point of what was new in the sacramental order introduced by Christ and carried forward by the body of Christ, the Church. Numbering the sacraments is a fruit of the Western tendency to usher mysteries into sheep-pens and shear them all over to make them nice and tidy. The body of Christ, however, is all sacrament, and everything that goes on in it is conditioned by that: even the church-cleaning and the meetings of the church council.

The Tree

So far we have traced the line of development from God's relation to his creation before Christ, through the dramatic change brought about by the incarnation, and on to the 'mystery' of the Church which emerged as a consequence, all the time keeping our eye on the phenomenon of structures and roles, and on how this affects our capacity to become persons. It is necessary, as we have seen, to make some distinction between Church structures as 'map' and the larger mystery of the Church, for God's sovereignty can never be pinned down to our satisfaction. In fact we see a phenomenon here which is recognizable too in any ordinary human groupings and in human society as a whole. If human societies naturally evolve structures, there are other things they evolve too to go along with the structures. Weaving amongst the structural ramifications is another phenomenon of a very different nature: spontaneous living, and living gifts. These are inseparable from the structures. One cannot live without the other, and both are needed. Life without structures gives us anarchy. The opposite, the attempt to have structures without life, was well illustrated in communist regimes: the system ran everything, spontaneity was stifled, and the result was disastrous. Structure and spontaneity need each other, but they are not comfortable bedfellows. At some points structure and freedom coincide harmoniously, but at others they live in a tension which can sometimes be intolerable. Most of the time the relationship is taut.

An illustration of this could be a tree. Rooted in things beyond our vision, it branches out and up into the air in all directions. Each branch stems from the trunk, each smaller branch from a larger one, and each twig from the smaller branches. The sap passes through to every twig and bud, and the whole intricate system bears leaves, blossom and fruit.

The branches, however, also embrace another world, that of life among the branches, the tree's ecosystem. Insects and grubs live and move in the bark; if they did not pollinate the blossom there would be no fruit. All manner of birds pass through, resting on the branches, sometimes making a home there. The leaves breathe the surrounding air, and the tree remains exposed to all the elements. The rain feeds its roots, and leaves its branches dripping and soaked; the wind prunes off bits and pieces as it pushes and sways it. The setting sun turns its mosses and lichens to vivid green, and its bark to red and gold. The tree is clearly distinguishable from the world which surrounds it: the ecosystem, however, is not so easily defined, and merges with the surrounding cosmos. The world of farther afield can be dangerous. A tree can be struck by lightning or felled by a woodman or blown over in a gale. Even those who depend on a tree, such as woodworm, can destroy it. The relationship with its world is not easy.

The tree is a parable of society. Structures of authority and relationship are so necessary to the whole enterprise that it cannot exist without them. They are, nevertheless, in tension with the sovereign spirit of life.

As an image of the Church, the tree itself represents all the baptized (we make no distinction here between laity and 'clergy'). The trunk and branches are equivalent to the organs in St Paul's image of the body. The tree is the necessary structure, and it is a living thing, growing and evolving all the time. It stands for those structures which the Church has succeeded in 'mapping' and, in the best sense, institutionalizing.

In and around the tree lives its ecosystem. This also is all the baptized, without distinction, the only difference being that now the borders are unknown – the ecosystem is part of the surrounding air, and it moves and blows about much more as it wants, even though still as a system, not as chaos. This image does not suggest anarchy alongside law, but a unity within which order and freedom co-inhabit. The ecosystem is that part of the Church's life which has eluded the mapmakers. The relationship between tree and ecosystem, as we have said, is taut.

> The key lies   at the
> point where   everything
> interlocks: 'tree' and
> 'life' dance   with
> each other,   and
> against one
>   another,
> taut and   tense;
> then just   flittingly
> theymergeintoonemystery,
>   before   dancing apart
>   once   more
>   till   next
>   they   come
>   towards   each
>   otherandthen
>   away   once
>   more   yet ...

This applies to many aspects of the Church: biblical studies, doctrine, ethics or ministry. But with this last topic we have to be careful. The tree is not to be identified with the clergy, but with all the baptized. The body of Christ lives in two modes: the first is as organs of the body, in which all according to their gifts are disposed in roles and vocations at many levels, some of them duplicating and overlapping. Then the second mode is as an ecosystem, including the clergy again, together with all Christian people, as they live the spontaneous side of their experience. In the midst of it all, we find today a disagreement as to what is distinctive about the bishop, priest and deacon.

Is the ministry unique?

For our generation the sacramental order can seem as far-fetched as magic. But then so does the incarnation and indeed God himself; and so we are brought back to faith. Once you enter upon the enterprise of believing in God, either you believe that he is a disengaged spectator, or you believe he is involved and active. Sacraments can be seen as an inevitable consequence of belief in God. They are certainly a logical consequence of it. We may have problems with a literal interpretation of the accounts of the incarnation in the New Testament, but we can quite easily accept that they fit admirably with the picture of God presented by Jesus, and that, were we God, it is what we would have wanted to do (had we the courage).

If you reject the incarnation, then it is difficult to believe in the sacramental order. If you accept the incarnation, then the sacramental order follows as a natural consequence. Otherwise, we would need to believe that the uniqueness of the bridge made by the incarnation was present here among us in Christ and then went away again, everything returning to a purely 'spiritual' level.

It is therefore possible to hold one of two points of view about the nature of the sacred ministry. One point of view, which traces its roots particularly to the Western Catholic tradition, wants to say that something essentially distinctive is conferred in ordination. The bishop and the priest, at least, are ontologically different from the rest of the faithful. The other point of view sees such a belief to be unreal or irrelevant. Some would go so far as to discourage even the kind of natural distinctions which arise in the secular world, and to say the clergy are no different in any way from anybody else. It is very easy to become bogged down in discussions of this type, and a reason for that is not very hard to find: in a culture as individualistic and as materialistic and functionalist as our own we are not in a good position to understand the question: in fact, we can hardly ask it without misunderstanding it, for we automatically think in terms of status rather than role, and of the individual rather than the community. We need to redress the balance by looking down the other end of our telescope, and ask another question: 'What is distinctive about the Church?'

The distinctiveness of the Church lies in the fact that she is sacrament, the sacrament of the body of Christ himself. Therefore everything is different. This 'everything' is partly expressed by an inner life articulated in a diversity of gifts: there is the gift of the baptized, the gift of bishops, the gift of church musicians, the gift of readers, the gift of priests, and so on. These gifts are not private possessions: they all weave together, all are branches of the vine, and coursing through them all is the same life of the Spirit. Only as part of a whole 'tree' can they be understood; and only as part of the 'life' amongst its branches, dancing together, weaving among one another, can we begin to see them for what they are.

Such an exalted vision of the Church can be mere triumphalism if the way we live does not match our words. We must always make a distinction between the vision held before us and our continual failure to be faithful to it. Yet it would be mere ideology if we tried to do it off our own bat. It will look preposterous unless it is the work of God. We can't simply aim that our parish church life set an example to the local community, and if we did people would see through it. All we can hope for is that we will be so faithful in our quest for the will of God for us that the sacramental vision of the body of Christ will be sensed through us. At the straightforward level of imitation and plain humanity the parish congregation often has as much to learn from the non-church community as vice versa. Our hands are empty. All we have to offer is God.

If the Church is indeed the sacrament of the incarnate and risen Lord, then we shall end with a very high doctrine indeed of all the roles in the Church, and of the baptized most of all. We shall not be worried about recognizing clear distinctions between them, for this is a lively body, not a soup, and it is a united body, not divided. All the gifts belong to all. The distinct gift and mystery of the priesthood 'belongs' not to the one to whom it has been entrusted, but to the whole Church, but it belongs to the whole Church *as it is exercised in that particular person.*

Deacons

Amongst all the gifts of the Church we need to say something further here about the diaconate. In Western experience diaconate and priesthood have been so closely bound together that the one can seem to be merely a watered-down form of the other. The deacon is then an apprentice priest, subject to certain temporary restrictions. Considerable effort has recently been devoted to identifying the distinctiveness of the diaconate, and, as John Collins's book *Diakonia*[4] has shown, there has been in recent years a great deal of over-simplification and misinterpretation of the terms 'ministry' and '*diakonia*' in general, resulting in a view of the Church's gifts as varying degrees of ministerial priesthood, a bit watered-down for deacons, and rather more so for other folk. Laity are to be more like priests, and the clergy more like layfolk. Paul's image of the organs of the body speaks of a distinctiveness which is much more radical. The gifts differ from each other not like different recipes for tomato soup, but as music differs from painting: the difference is enormous and fundamental, and yet both are about exactly the same business, and their coming together can have devastating effects. So with the difference between priest and deacon – the deacon's vocation has a flavour and genius all of its own. It is as difficult to put into words as the priesthood, and its character stands out most in the liturgy, in pastoral work and in the internal life of the Christian community. The fact that we have problems in identifying what a deacon is may perhaps be telling us that there is something wrong with our liturgy and with the fabric of parish community.

Conclusions

The ministerial priesthood takes its place in the dance of the people of God. Here we have not any old roles, but an articulated ensemble which is all sacrament. To be sure, we see the kind of personnel structures found, say, in an army or a district council: the roles fulfil a *function*, particular *values* come to be attributed to them, they influence *character*, their holders can come to be closely *identified* with them, and they can function as a powerful *symbol*. But all of this is lifted into the sacramental order and transformed. There are clergy who claim they are no different from anybody else, but that is a claim they are not free to make. On the other hand, simply to say the priesthood is *ontologically* distinct is an unhelpful distortion. All we can do is 'map' what we can, and accept that we can only see as human beings see, not as God sees.

In this light we can begin to address the question which now beckons for attention: 'Who is the priest?'

Notes

1. H.B.Green CR, 'Apostolic Succession and the Anglican Appeal to History', *Church Quarterly Review* 163 (1962), p.301. (The quotation is from Austin Farrer, *The Apostolic Ministry*, Preface to the 1957 edition, p. vi.)
2. M.Santer, 'The Reconciliation of Memories', in Santer, ed., *Their Lord and Ours*, SPCK, 1982, pp.149-60.
3. *Unitatis redintegratio*, London: in G. Alberigo and N. Tanner SJ, ed., *Decrees of the Ecumenical Councils*, vol.2, London: Sheed & Ward, 1990, p.913.
4. John N. Collins, *Diakonia: Re-interpreting the Ancient Sources*, Oxford: Oxford University Press, 1990.

CHAPTER THREE

Who is the priest?

St Peter's supported a mission in a remote country in Africa and Kevin was sent with a group of young people for a short visit.

'Are there many people round here who aren't Christian?' he asked Alan, who together with his wife Ruth ran the mission.

'Plenty,' said Alan, 'I can take you to see some if you like. There is a wonderful people who live up in those hills, called the Uduli. Their life has remained unchanged for centuries. If you like, you can go with Father Jacob next time he goes on trek – you can make a short detour to call on them.'

So it was that one morning in November he was sitting in sweltering heat talking to the chief of the Uduli.

'Who is your father?' asked the chief.

'He is Stan,' replied Kevin ingenuously.

'Oh. But *who* is he?' Father Jacob translated all this with great patience.

'Well, I'm not sure I know what you're asking. I can tell you *what* he is.'

'But I know what he is,' said the chief, 'he is a man, who looks after his wife and children, provides their home and shelter, and plays his part in the community.'

'Well, what I mean,' said Kevin, nonplussed, 'is that he is a bus driver.'

Father Jacob paused for thought at this one, and then did the best he could with added gestures to indicate the size of the bus.

'But what does that do for him?' asked the chief, greatly puzzled. 'Why does he want to move this great big thing around all day?'

'Ah, well, he takes people in it to places that they want to go to.'

The chief's face brightened: 'Ah yes, now I begin to see, that is who he is. But what do they do for him?'

'They give him money.' Father Jacob endeavoured to explain that.

'But who made this money for them?'

Kevin explained that some people gave all their time to making it. The chief now laughed. 'How strange you people are! Why didn't you say this at the beginning – this is just what I wanted to know.' Kevin scratched his head, bemused. 'Now, Kevin, tell me where he got his bus and how he looks after it.'

'Oh the bus isn't his – it belongs to some other people.'

The chief laughed again. '*More* people? And how do they and your father belong to each other?'

'Er – well – my father sort of promises to go every day, and he gets some of the money.'

The chief now looked very pleased.

'But you haven't asked me who my mother is,' said Kevin, trying to take the initiative. His interlocutor looked very puzzled at this. So he pressed on quickly: 'My mother works in a shop.' The chief looked at him. 'The shop is like the bus, only people come there to get their clothes.'

The old man stroked his chin: 'Your father takes people around in a bus, the bus belongs to some more people,' he started counting it all on his fingers with increasing mirth; 'So he gets money made for him by yet more people,' he was trying to keep back his convulsions, 'while your mother helps people get their clothes, which are made by other people for her, that is, for them,' he said, now almost beside himself, 'and she too gains money made by the same people who made it,' he could now hardly speak, 'for the people who own the bus your father takes around'; he was unable to continue, the tears were rolling down his cheeks, as he howled with laughter. Father Jacob was a cheerful chap, if rather quiet, but now he too became helpless with laughter, though he had no idea what at.

The chief sobered up unexpectedly. 'Kevin, you must continually remember who you are, and who your father is. If you forget it, you will disappear. Your father is all these people. Without them, what he does is meaningless. Learn a new question. It is a matter of life and death to ask who a person is. My neighbour is who I am.'

After they had made their departure the chief remarked to his wife, 'These white men are a rum lot – they don't seem to realize who they are'.

At coffee on the following Sunday morning Kevin was full of it all. What a pity the Uduli were so far away. Better for them, though, on second thoughts. He caught a glimpse of Kath and remembered her prod at his sermon. How could anyone think Africa could make us patronizing?

'I bet I know what you're thinking,' she said. 'But just think – God is the clergy's daily Africa – and look what they make of him.' Kath had a heart of gold under the waspish exterior – Kevin wondered how he could work on her. Unfortunately she got so many things right.

Shepherding is perhaps the commonest image of priesthood throughout the Christian tradition, however strange it is to us today. But you cannot say much about shepherds without mentioning sheep; and, as the previous chapter has made clear, the same is true of ordained priests.[1] There's no getting at what they are without talking about the whole Church. And that is true in two senses. Priests are Christians before they are priests; so whatever is special about Christians, or about the whole body of Christians, the Church, will apply to priests too. And second, priests do not live and work in isolation; they relate to a community. So any attempt to say what is distinctive about who they are and what they do will involve talking about everyone else as well. So in this chapter too, even if the spotlight is on the ordained priesthood – the shepherds – we shall also be saying something about the sheep.

Perhaps that makes the business of priesthood look complicated before we have even begun. And there is something else that certainly increases the difficulty. No human activity is completely unchanging. Modern shepherds certainly have something in common with their predecessors a hundred or even a thousand years ago. But there are also differences – and what goes for shepherds goes for the priesthood too. Perhaps each age likes to look on itself as a period when some really decisive changes occurred. The twentieth century can certainly make a strong claim; and it would be foolish to suppose that changes, whether in society or in the Church, do not have any impact on the priesthood. We have inherited a picture of the life and work of the priest within the Christian community from a time when all priests were full-time and male; their flocks were much more likely to live in stable, semi-agricultural communities than is the case now. In attempting to write about priesthood *today*, there is a real challenge to be faced in producing an account that is not so gender- or culture-specific as to be useless; an account that has something to say to Ministers in Secular Employment (MSEs) and to women now preparing for ordination to the priesthood in the Church of England, as well as to men in full-time stipendiary ministry.

More than just doing things

Faced by these difficulties – and by the strangeness of the whole notion of the Church and of sacrament to the modern mind – there is a terrible temptation to clutch at what is familiar. Priesthood is a job, isn't it? So why do we not simply write a job description – a list of all the things a priest is supposed to do? Then we would understand what priesthood today amounts to. And some modern discussions of priesthood are little more than this; a long list of activities that make up the priest's work, with perhaps a hint or two of the sort of secular job that priesthood most resembles. So perhaps we can think of the priest as a sort of manager. Priests are responsible for some plant (the church buildings); they direct a workforce (the congregation); and they are supposed to produce something: a mixture of church services popular enough to keep the church finances in order, and counselling and support for certain vulnerable sectors of society – the sick, the elderly, the bereaved and so on. They are accountable to senior managers in each region, called bishops, whose job it is to promote efficiency by rewarding successful clergy and chivvying those with out-of-date working practices.

This sort of caricature is easy enough to write, and it does not mean that there are no useful parallels to be drawn between priesthood and management, or that priests have nothing to learn from managers. The previous chapter made clear that there are roles evolved by the Church and those found in human institutions, and this holds good for priesthood. But at the same time the caricature does suggest that there is a certain inappropriateness in tackling the question 'What is priesthood today?' using only the tools that would be used to analyse much secular employment. The same sense of unease is generated even by a simple list of what a priest does. The priest baptizes, presides at the communion, absolves; visits the sick and the dying; perhaps does assemblies or a little teaching in the local schools; preaches; and so on. But how much has that actually told us? Not enough, and for two reasons. In the first place, many of the activities listed are not distinctive of priesthood in the sense that only ordained priests can or should do them. Many lay people visit the sick and the housebound. Clergy have no monopoly on school assemblies. Lay preaching is well established. Second, a simple list of what a priest does (or even of what *only* a priest can do) seems somehow to miss the essence of priesthood. It does not tell us why it should be these particular things that a priest does (they are a pretty odd assortment at first sight). What is at the heart of priestly life, holding it all together? Surely there's more to priesthood than doing things?

A couple of comparisons will make this point clearer. There are some jobs that can be adequately explained simply by describing the activities involved in doing them. A boot-boy shines shoes; a greengrocer sells fruit and vegetables; a window-cleaner cleans windows. You cannot call someone who cuts the grass a lawn-mower, but that is only because the machine got the word first, not because there is some further reality to cutting the grass that the word leaves out. But some other jobs are very different. You could make a list of all the things that a teacher does: preparing lessons, going through them in class, marking pupils' work, supervising breaks, and the rest of it. But even if you made a list much longer and much more technical than that one, you would still not have captured what it is to be a teacher. Teaching is not just about doing things; it involves the communication of a whole set of attitudes and values. That in turn is bound up with the sort of person you are (it is often said that you can pick a teacher out straightaway at a party, or on holiday); as you learn to be a teacher, not least through teaching, your character is moulded. Teaching involves many aspects of the person. That is why, unlike grass-cutting, or shoe-cleaning, we cannot really imagine the job being taken over by a machine. There are plenty of other examples of jobs like this. Doctors, nurses, soldiers, social workers: in all these cases, just listing the activities the job involves does not get you very far. All these jobs involve the whole personality; they involve being a certain sort of person. And the same is true of priesthood.

These arguments suggest that the question we should be asking is not (or at least, not only) 'What does a priest do?' but rather, 'What *is* a priest?' If you are a priest, what sort of person does that mean being? But as soon as we ask that question, especially if we are in search of what is *distinctive* about being a priest, we need to be aware of a danger, the danger of treating the priest as somebody completely different and separate from any other Christian. If we want to know what sort of person the priest is called to be, we need to know first what sort of person any Christian is called to be, for being a priest is not just something that involves the whole person; it is also a calling that is exercised within the distinctive context of the Church. As we noted at the start of this chapter, a priest is a Christian before being a priest. Priests therefore, like all Christians, share in and contribute to the distinctive sacramental character of the whole Church as outlined in the previous chapter. And they share too the calling of any Christian to become a 'real person' after the pattern of Christ.

In Christ's image

Christian personality – what it is to be a Christian – and the distinctive sacramental character of the Church are both rooted in baptism. In baptism, according to St Paul, we share Christ's death so that we may come to share his life also (Rom. 6; Col. 2). This participation in Christ maintains the Church as sacrament; through the Church's sharing in Christ's life and death in baptism, the bridge between God and humanity made in Christ is continued. And it is in baptism too, by our union with Christ, the one true person, that each of us sets out on the path to discovering the 'real me'. We abandon our old selfish ways; a new personality is born and grows in us, a personality that is to be the image of Christ, sharing his pattern of death and resurrection. This sharing in Christ's death and in his resurrection is no trivial matter. Our transformation is to be complete, and that scale of change involves the pain and suffering that characterize death. It is not a case of a lick of paint and a roll or two of new wallpaper – a weekend DIY job. It is more like a thorough rebuilding – structural repairs, re-plastering, decorating and all – for our task as Christians is 'to grow up in *every way* into him who is the head, into Christ' (Eph. 4.15); to 'put on the new nature, created after the likeness of God in true righteousness and holiness' (Eph. 4.24); so that Paul can even claim that 'it is no longer I who live, but Christ who lives in me' (Gal. 2.20).

This growth into true personhood, into being the 'real me', is not an obstacle course we complete by our own strength, or a hidden truth we search out by our own intellect. No: as the first chapter repeatedly stressed, becoming a true person is something we receive as a *gift*. It is said that by God's grace we are enabled to become persons in the sense in which Christ was a person, and so to be 'partakers of the divine nature' (2 Pet. 1.4). This gift is offered to every Christian, and so also to priests. But of course, no two Christians are identical; and it is here that we can begin to speak of what makes priests different.

Every Christian is called to grow up into the likeness of Christ; but the way in which each Christian does this is different. People image Christ in different ways. What is more, they do not do this in isolation, quite separately from each other. On the contrary: since all are baptized into the one Christ, all Christians form one body (1 Cor. 12), and it is the existence within this one body of different ways of growing into the likeness of Christ, of becoming true persons, that both enables each member of the body to achieve that likeness and preserves the unity of that body. We should not imagine the Church as a garden of exotic flowers with each bloom making its own vivid impression quite independently of the rest. A flower arrangement is much nearer the mark, where the impression made by each plant depends to some extent on all the rest, the idea being that all combine together to make a single arrangement. Or we can return to St Paul's image of the body:

> His gifts were that some should be apostles, some
> prophets, some evangelists, some pastors and

teachers, to equip the saints for the work of ministry, for building up the body of Christ, until we all attain to the unity of the faith and of the knowledge of the Son of God, to mature manhood, to the measure of the stature of the fullness of Christ. (Eph. 4.11-13)

Priests, like all other Christians, are called to grow up into the likeness of Christ within the one body, the Church; but they are called to resemble Christ in a particular way, for the sake of the whole. What sort of person is a priest? A person whose life is one particular image of Christ, lived together with, and for the sake of, fellow Christians.

New Testament priesthood

This view of priesthood is underlined by an examination of the New Testament understanding of priesthood. It is well known that the New Testament only very occasionally applies the term 'priest' (Greek *hiereus*) to any individual other than Christ, and this has sometimes been seen as a fatal objection to any exercise of priestly ministry by individual Christians. Certainly Christian priests have not always avoided seeing their priesthood as an individual possession, a private privilege, in a way that flies in the face of the New Testament understanding of priesthood. But the New Testament view is more subtle and profound than a simple rejection of such ministry. The primary use of priestly language and imagery in the New Testament is with reference to Christ. He is seen (above all in the Letter to the Hebrews, but also in the sacrificial imagery of Revelation and of the story of the Passion in the Gospel of John) as both priest and sacrificial victim. By the offering of his whole life of sinless obedience to God, culminating in his death on the cross, he has brought about a decisive and complete reconciliation between humanity and God. But there is a second New Testament usage of priestly language. In the First Letter of Peter, the Christian body is exhorted to be 'a spiritual priesthood (Greek *hierateuma*) to offer spiritual sacrifices acceptable to God through Jesus Christ'; they are 'a chosen race, a royal priesthood (Greek *hierateuma*), a holy nation' (1 Pet. 2.5,9). These comments come in a passage about baptism. They suggest that the whole Christian body is called to be priestly, a priesthood dependent on the priesthood of Christ. Because we are joined to Christ in baptism, and called to grow into his likeness, one way in which we are to resemble him is by being priestly. The whole Church, *as a body*, is called to image in its life Christ's life of obedient sacrifice. And the few references that there are in the New Testament to Christians as 'priests' (Greek *hiereis*) share this corporate emphasis. In Revelation, Christians are twice (1.6; 5.10) described as 'a kingdom, priests' (Greek *hiereis*) to God in a phrase drawing on Old Testament usage (Exodus 19.6, Isaiah 61.6); the same Old Testament language lies behind the description of those who share in the first resurrection as 'priests (Greek *hiereis*) of God and of Christ' in Revelation 20.6. But just as in the Old Testament passages it is the whole people of Israel that is seen as priestly, so in Revelation priesthood is seen not as a possession of every Christian, taken as an individual, but as something that the whole body shares; and shares in dependence on Christ and the salvation that his sacrifice brought.

Any other sort of Christian priesthood, if it is to be faithful to the New Testament, must fit in with the New Testament picture of Christ as the only priest in the full sense of the term, and of the whole Christian body as priestly in a secondary sense, dependent on Christ. It must be a particular ministry that is derived from Christ and promotes the priesthood of the whole body. And it is exactly this that our discussion of baptism, of what it is to be a Christian person, suggests. Every Christian life depends on Christ. Together in the one body we each grow up in our particular way into the likeness of Christ. If one of these ways of being a Christian person is to be an ordained priest, that way of being will be priestly not by usurping the priesthood of Christ or of the whole body, but by offering a likeness of the priesthood of Christ in a life of sacrifice that makes Christ present and so helps the whole body fulfil its vocation to be a royal priesthood.

St Paul, whose ministry well fits this pattern, once described himself as a 'minister of Christ Jesus in the priestly service of the gospel of God' (Rom. 15.16). Priestly terminology for this particular ministry in the Church became common only after New Testament times, and as we have seen in Chapter 2, it took some time for the distinctiveness of the ordained ministry to emerge. But priesthood is more than a matter of terminology, and the origins of priestly ministry, and some of its key characteristics, are to be found in the New Testament, albeit not fully developed. Paul's understanding of his own ministry is of crucial importance here: he sees his apostolate as a gift of God, (1 Cor. 1.1; 2 Cor. 1.1; Gal. 1.1) given to enable the ministry of Christ to continue:

> All this is from God, who through Christ reconciled us to himself and gave us the ministry of reconciliation; that is, God was in Christ reconciling the world to himself, not counting their trespasses against them, and entrusting to us the message of reconciliation. So we are ambassadors for Christ, God making his appeal through us. We beseech you on behalf of Christ, be reconciled to God. (2 Cor. 5.18-20)

Here is a priestly ministry in embryo: a ministry given by God, dependent on Christ, and furthering the reconciliation with God that he brought about through a life that follows the pattern of his life.

A similar understanding of ministry as a gift given to some in particular for the sake of all, and dependent on the ministry of Christ, is to be found in the Gospels. 'As the Father has sent me, even so I send you,' says the risen Christ to his disciples (John 20.21); compare the accounts of the commissioning of the twelve (Matt. 10; Luke 9). And in the Acts of the Apostles we see the apostles (Greek *apostoloi* – 'those sent') fulfilling Christ's commission to them: teaching and breaking bread with their fellow Christians, and proclaiming the kingdom of God and the victory of Christ by their preaching, healing and baptizing in his name (see Acts 2). The doctrine of the 'apostolic succession' should not be seen simply as a claim that a chain of laying on of hands can be traced back without a break to the apostles (a claim which, as we have already seen, remains a matter of uncertainty in the 'tunnel period' before it came to have canonical status); it points rather to the fact that ordained priests today continue the work of the apostles, and stand in the tradition of ministry that was initiated by Christ through the apostles. There is evidence at least in the case of St Paul that he took considerable care to hand his work on to reliable successors (see his speech to the elders of the church at Ephesus in Acts 20).

So it is here that the New Testament roots of the ordained

priesthood lie, in descriptions of actual ministries sharing the character of Christ's priesthood (whether exercised by apostles, presbyters or *episkopoi* [overseers]), as much as in passages containing explicitly priestly terminology. Those passages, however, do stand as a reminder of what our consideration of baptism made clear. Ordained priesthood, like any other particular way of being a baptized Christian, exists in dependence on Christ and in and for the sake of the whole body.

A *certain sort of person*

The priest, then, is called not in the first place to *do* certain things, but rather to *be* something: a person who reflects the person of Christ, and grows into his likeness, in a distinctive way that builds up the whole body of the Church. And it is at least partly because priesthood is about being a certain sort of person, not just performing certain functions, that ordination has traditionally been seen as permanent. Once a priest, always a priest, because priesthood affects the sort of person you are in a way that cannot simply be laid aside. But the time has come to say in some more detail just what sort of person a priest is called to be. What does this particular way of growing into the likeness of Christ, of becoming a 'real person', involve?

This question is best answered in two parts, for there are two basic sides to the business of being a priest: making Christ present to others, and being a public example of a Christian. But you cannot have one without the other; the two sides of Christian priesthood belong together, like the two sides of a door (you could not very well have a door with only one side). One of the things that holds them together is that both aspects of being a priest exist in relation to and for the sake of the rest of Christ's body, the Church. (It was a desire to underline this, and to avoid any temptation to regard priesthood as a means of giving an exalted status to the individual priest, that motivated the insistence of the Council of Chalcedon, maintained in the present Church of England, that no one may be ordained priest without having a specific Christian community to relate to as pastor.) Other ways in which the two basic aspects of priesthood form a unity will become clear later; but for now, we shall take them in turn.

Making Christ present

First of all, then, priests are called to be people who make Christ present to his people. By who they are and what they do, priests are the means through which Christ's own priestly ministry becomes a reality for each congregation. It is not that Christ is otherwise absent (for he is present in a great variety of ways in all the baptized faithful), but the particular way in which the priest is called to make that presence evident and effective also helps us to see Christ at work elsewhere – just as church buildings, rather than being the *only* places where we can find God, help us to find God outside. (Similarly, looking at flowers in a botanical garden makes you better at recognizing them in the wild.) For, as argued in Chapter 2, God in Christ remains vitally present in the Church and so available to the world. This presence is a gift given to the whole Church; priests are the means by which it is given, not through their own power, but through Christ working in them ('without me you can do nothing', John 15.5).

Priests speak in Christ's name; they preach his gospel; they bring his blessing, his forgiveness, his presence to the people whom they serve. There are of course specific actions by which this is done, above all by the preaching and expounding of the gospel and the celebration of the sacraments. But it is also true that the whole life of the priest must be one which makes the love of Christ a reality for each person with whom the priest comes into contact. And this love may on occasion be expressed in the most ordinary ways – in five minutes' conversation at a bus-stop, or by the changing of a light bulb for somebody who has no one else to ask – as well as by the celebration of the sacraments. Something of this is captured by the famous prayer of St Teresa of Avila: 'Christ has now no hands on earth but yours, no feet to go about doing good but yours . . .'

The priest is not a mere illustration of Christ and his love, nor again an essentially mechanical device for distributing God's grace, like a slot-machine. Rather, the priest's whole life, whether in liturgy, preaching or pastoral care, is called both to be a sign of Christ's love and to make present that which it signifies. It is this that makes it possible to speak of ordination as a sacrament, for living signs are what the sacraments are. The bread and wine at the Eucharist are not, to borrow a vivid phrase of P.T.Forsyth, 'merely striking visual aids in principle classifiable with film-strips'; they make present that which they signify, the body and blood of Christ. In the same way the life of a priest must make a reality of the love of Christ, above all of his offering of himself in obedience to the Father, and of the reconciliation that that brought about. And this sacramentality of priesthood reminds us again that priests, like any other sacrament, do not exist in isolation and for themselves, but in and for the people of God. Priesthood exists to equip the Church in its turn to be a sacrament – a sacrament of God's love for the world.

The first aspect of what it is to be a priest is given clear expression in the ASB Ordinal (or service for the ordination of priests) in the Declaration read by the bishop before the actual ordination. The bishop there reminds those to be ordained priest that they are called 'to grow up into his [the Lord's] likeness, and sanctify the lives of all with whom [they] have to do'. In the Declaration, the bishop sets out certain tasks that those ordained priest must perform, some very specific (such as baptizing, preparing the baptized for confirmation and presiding at the Holy Communion), others more general (leading the people in prayer and worship and caring for them). But the Declaration makes it plain that, as was argued above, priesthood involves more than just *doing* things. 'We trust', says the bishop to those to be ordained, 'that you are fully determined, by the grace of God, to give yourselves *wholly* to his service'; and the Declaration moves from setting out certain of the tasks of a priest to a consideration of *what sort of person* a priest must be. Of what sort of person, of what way of being, are the specific tasks mentioned a characteristic expression?

Images of priesthood

The way the Declaration answers this question, and sets out what it is to be a priest, is by offering a series of images of priesthood. The modern mind is on occasion very suspicious of this sort of approach – why can we not dispense with the images and simply set everything out in black and white? But in fact we use images all the time, and for the good reason that they have a depth and suggestiveness to them, an ability to involve our hearts as well as our heads, that we cannot do without. So, at a fairly superficial level, we often talk of our politicians in sporting terms (they tackle each other, try to keep the ball in play, and often end up scoring own goals), or envisage the country as a ship, battered by economic storms which it tries to weather in order to stay on course. And less superficially, the images we use of our own lives, or of other people, tell us a good deal about how we think and feel. Do you imagine your life as a journey (where are you trying to get to?) or as a puzzle (something that has to be solved) or even as a board game (making the right moves in a competition that you have to win)? And just think how much you can suggest about a person by saying that he is a donkey, or mulish, or mouse-like. Or a wolf.

Once we realize how pervasive images are in our language, and how powerful, it will come as no surprise that they are also the stuff of religion. The Bible is full of them. Think, for instance, of the wealth of images used to convey something of the reality of God. God is seen as father, king and judge; as warrior and lover; as a consuming fire and a still small voice; as a gardener and a shepherd. These images cannot be built up, or reduced, into one straightforward picture; indeed, they are to some extent in conflict. But taken together, *as images*, they show us something of God. Similarly with the Church. One New Testament image for the Church which has been prominent in our discussions is that of the body. There are others: the Church is a building, a household, a vine. These images cannot be added up, they do not fit together into a single picture. But each of them reveals something of what the Church is, in a way that a plain statement could not.

The same is true of the images of priesthood offered in the Ordinal. They too are scriptural images, images in many cases used of Christ. They suggest what priests are called to *be*, what it will be for them to be 'real persons', and that their actions must spring from this reality. Insofar as they are images first used of Christ, they underline the call to priests to make real the presence of Christ to his people, which we have identified as the first aspect of a priestly life. This is above all true of the first two images of priesthood offered by the Declaration in the Ordinal: 'The priest is called by God to work with the bishop ... as servant and shepherd among the people to whom he is sent.' Servant and shepherd. Both these images are applied by Christ to himself in the Gospels. Checking the ambition of his disciples in Mark 10, Jesus concludes: 'The Son of Man also came not to be served but to serve, and to give his life as a ransom for many' (Mark 10.45). The image is given a more concrete presentation by John in his description of Jesus washing the feet of his disciples on the eve of his passion. As applied to priesthood, the image suggests the quality of humble labour for others, in obedience to the Father, and to the point of sacrificing one's own life, that must characterize the life of the priest. This is one of the realities of Christ's life into which priests must seek to grow, and thus make it present for their people.

The image of the shepherd is even more central: the Declaration insists that the priest 'must set the Good Shepherd always before him as the pattern of his calling, caring for the people committed to his charge'. The image of the shepherd may seem distant from most people's experience in modern Britain (arguably it was no closer to the experience of the first Christians, who were largely urban); in any case, the force of this image is less to be found in our knowledge of sheep-farming than in the use made of it in the Gospel of John. The use of the image there draws on a long tradition of biblical imagery. The Lord is often spoken of in the Old Testament as the shepherd of his people (e.g. Ps. 80.1 'Give ear, O Shepherd of Israel, thou who leadest Joseph like a flock!'); the use of the image is extended to the leaders of Israel under God (as, for example, in the sharp criticisms expressed in Ezekiel 34 of shepherds who look to their own advantage and not that of the flock, or in the promise in Jeremiah 23.4 'I will set shepherds over them who will care for them'). In John 10 Jesus draws on this tradition to portray himself as the Good Shepherd – the faithful leader of his people through whom God's guidance and care is expressed. But he develops and transforms the image by his insistence that the supreme act of the shepherd is to lay down his life for the sheep. What then does the application of this image to priesthood suggest that priests are called to be? People who grow to be like Christ in their faithful service of their flocks even to the point of sacrificing their own lives. Priests are to know their people; to foster their unity; to give them life, and abundantly; to lay down their lives for them. In so doing they will mirror the life of obedience and sacrifice of Christ, and so make that a reality among those whom they serve.

Messengers, watchmen and stewards

Other images are also suggested by the Ordinal. Priests are to be the 'messengers, watchmen and stewards of the Lord'. In some respects the ideas evoked by these images overlap with those suggested by 'servant' and 'shepherd' and discussed above. A steward is a kind of servant especially concerned with the distribution of the master's food. So also the priest is called to feed the Lord's people in his name with his word and his sacraments. One thing all the images have in common is that they are all relational in the sense that they involve someone else – the sheep who will be tended, those to whom the servant will minister and whom the steward will feed, those whom the watchman will warn and to whom the messenger will speak. Once again it is underlined that priests, in bringing the reality of Christ to their people, must live not for themselves but for others, as he did.

The last image – that of the messenger – suggests a part of the priestly task of bringing Christ to his people that is less prominent in the images of 'servant' and 'shepherd'. Jesus came from God, was sent by God, to bring good news to his people, the good news of his kingdom. So also priests are called to be bearers of good news, not only in what they say but in what their whole life proclaims about the love of God. Here again they speak and act in the Lord's name, and so make him present. This image of the messenger, and its associated task of preaching the kingdom, is no less central to the ministry of a priest than the tasks associated with the images of shepherd and steward discussed above. Proclaiming the word of the Lord is identified again and again in the ASB Ordinal as a key part of what it is to be a priest, and at the foundations of the ordained priesthood we find the preaching of Jesus and his disciples in the Gospels, of the apostles in Acts, and of Paul in his epistles. If ordained priests cease to be the messengers of the Lord, there is a risk that their ministry will become deadeningly churchy, committed simply to the Church as institution. But there is a contrary danger. The public nature of priesthood inevitably means that priests are called upon to speak to the world in the name of the Church, and this may indeed be an opportunity for being the Lord's messengers. But it is also crucial to recall the relationship of the priesthood of the ordained ministry to the royal priesthood of the whole body of the Church. Both are dependent on the priesthood of Christ; and the former exists to serve the latter. Priests are not called to do the work of the rest of the Church on its behalf, but their ministry does exist, in Paul's words, 'to equip the saints for the work of ministry, for building up the body of Christ' (Eph. 4.12). That is to say, ordained priests are called to ensure by their proclamation of the Lord's message that the Church is equipped to proclaim this to the world – not to attempt to take on the Church's task of proclamation single-handedly themselves. This does not of course mean that they will not on occasion be involved in mission – quite the contrary, especially in areas where the Church barely exists. But much of the time, their task will rather be to equip others for mission.

We have dwelt at some length on the images of priesthood offered in the Ordinal as part of our examination of the first aspect of the life of a priest, the vocation to grow into the sort of likeness to Christ that makes him present to his people, and so reveals to them what it really is to be a person. By making Christ present in the Church, such priesthood indeed helps the Church fulfil its vocation to be sacramental, to make Christ really present to the world. The images have helped reveal priesthood as a call to be a certain sort of person in and for the body of Christ, rather than simply to do certain jobs.

The assertion in the same context that people are *called by God* to priesthood, that priesthood is a matter of *vocation*, suggests the same conclusion. If priesthood were simply a matter of doing certain jobs on behalf of the Church, it would be natural to think of priests as no more than people delegated by the Church to certain functions from time to time. But priesthood is a matter of becoming a certain sort of person; and it is by the gift of God that any Christian is enabled to grow into personhood, and it is God's call and that person's response that initiates the growth.

The second aspect of the life of a priest, to which we shall shortly turn, is more straightforward. But before leaving the images of the Ordinal, something must be said of three problems, not confined to the images, but highlighted by them.

Priests and bishops

The first of these is the relation between priesthood and episco-pate. How do priests differ from bishops? The problem is suggested by the images because they are often applied as much to bishops as to priests; although the Declaration discussed above comes from the Ordination of Priests, the images that make it up are derived from the New Testament, in which no consistent distinction between priests (Greek *presbyteroi*) and bishops (Greek *episkopoi*) is made. The time it took for these ministries to develop and become distinct has been noted above; in origin they have a common root. This suggests that differences between bishops and priests do not run very deep: their vocations are in many respects very similar. In essence, priests are assistants and representatives of the bishop (with whom, as the Declaration insists, they are called to work); bishops in ordaining priests, empower them for certain of their own functions (such as teaching and celebrating the Eucharist), but other functions (in the Church of England, ordination and confirmation) are normally reserved to the bishop. Like priests, bishops also are called to make Christ's presence among their people a reality by their life and work.

The bishop, as the chief pastor of each diocese, has a particular responsibility for the unity of that diocese, and of the whole Church; but that in turn reminds us of a side of priestly ministry that has not yet been much discussed. The priest too must be an agent of unity, not only in each congregation and parish, but also between congregations. Priests are called and sent by God; the Church acknowledges and guides that vocation. As assistants of the bishop, whose ministry is recognized by the whole Church, priests are called to build unity between their people and the whole body of the Church. In doing this they again make present the person of Christ. For, 'in him all things hold together' (Col. 1.17); he 'is our peace, who has made us both one, and has broken down the dividing wall of hostility' (Eph. 2.14). (We may note in passing that this is one element of what it is to be a priest that raises questions about certain modern forms of Anglican priesthood. The concept of the Local Ordained Minister (LOM) gives clear expression to the close bond between priest and people – priests are called from within the Church. But it is not yet clear that it adequately embodies the universality of the Church of which the priest is both a representative and a nurturer, nor the truth that the priest is sent, as well as called.)

Complete commitment

A second problem is raised by the emphasis of the images on the
need for a priest to be a certain sort of person, rather than just to
perform certain functions – something on which we have laid
considerable stress. What the images suggest – that priesthood
involves complete commitment of the whole person – the
Ordinal explicitly enjoins, especially in the Book of Common
Prayer:

> We have good hope ... that you have clearly deter-
> mined, by God's grace, to give yourselves wholly to
> this office, whereunto it hath pleased God to call you:
> so that, as much as lieth in you, you will apply
> yourselves wholly to this one thing, and draw all your
> cares and studies this way.

It is clear enough that priesthood involves all the capacities of
those called to it – mental, physical, emotional, spiritual. In this
it is no different from the vocation of any of the baptized: all are
called to become persons in the sense in which Christ is a true
person, by growing into his likeness, and this cannot involve
anything less than our complete humanity. It is, however, less
clear exactly what constraints this puts on the sort of lives that
priests can lead. The medieval Western Church, and the modern
Roman Church of the Latin rite, have seen priesthood as normally involving a commitment to celibacy; other churches,
including the Church of England since the Reformation, have
reached the different conclusion that this is for the individual
priest to decide. Each age raises its own questions of this sort;
one that is at present being debated in the Church of England
concerns Ministers in Secular Employment (MSEs, formerly
Non-Stipendiary Ministers). Evidence suggests that it was a
common enough pattern in the very early church for those
ordained to retain a full-time job, but since that period priests
have not normally been expected to have other work. If, as we
have argued, priesthood indeed involves a whole pattern of life,
and is one way of growing into the likeness of Christ, lived in
relation to a Christian community, we need to discover what this
might mean for priests who spend much of their time in a workplace that may have little or no Christian identity, and then have to

relate to a congregation that may be quite separate. There are no easy answers to this sort of question; it will take time to assess the development of priesthood that MSEs represent, and whether there are any aspects of priesthood to which full-time secular employment makes it impossible to do justice.

Women and priesthood

The third problem raised by the New Testament images of priesthood set out in the Ordinal goes even deeper and also allows no immediate solution. We stressed at the beginning of this chapter our desire to offer an account of priesthood that was not gender-specific; not restricted by the terms in which it was expressed to men. Our general statement of the first aspect of priesthood – the sacramental presentation of Christ to his people through growth into a particular likeness of him – perhaps satisfies this desire. But it is plain that much of the New Testament imagery used in the Ordinal to give depth to this aspect of priesthood is associated primarily with men. This is not only a matter of the words used. They are problematic ('watchmen' is the most obviously masculine, but could perhaps be replaced by a neutral term such as 'watcher'; 'shepherdess' and 'stewardess' (!) hardly have the same connotations as 'shepherd' and 'steward'; 'messenger' and 'servant' are more neutral). But in a way much more problematic is the inescapable fact that throughout their history these images have been used only of men, and developed with only men in mind.

One response to this would be to deny that the images can have any further value if the priesthood is genuinely to be open to women. But they are so central to the tradition of the ordained priesthood that any account of priesthood that excludes them risks in its turn being cut off from that tradition, and so becoming even more partial. It is better to note that neither priesthood, nor the images associated with it, are static. This is indeed true of the life of the individual priest: each priest finds that, although priesthood in one sense began at the moment of ordination, in another the vocation began much earlier than that, and the response to it, the growth into priesthood, continues through ordination. Priests are shaped by the people they serve: here again the mutuality of the ordained priesthood and the rest of the body of Christ is evident.

Similarly, priesthood has developed through Christian history, in part in response to the circumstances in which people have lived and worked as priests. This suggests that as women are ordained and start to live as priests, that will in time affect the nature of priesthood and our understanding of it.

New images may be developed (some modern images of priesthood have been suggested: speech therapy is one). The traditional images may be reinterpreted. That this process is one of development will ensure that, in the changes, the essence of what it is to be a priest will not be lost. It is impossible to anticipate this process. Perhaps the best that can be done is to offer an account, as we have tried to do, that grounds the images in a general understanding of the first aspect of priestly life that is not gender-specific (growth into that particular likeness of Christ that makes him present to his people) and then to recognize that the images that go with this, crucial as they are, will be bound to be subject to development in the next decades.

Christians in the public eye

The ordination of women to the priesthood also has a bearing on the second aspect of what it is to be a priest, though in a much less problematic fashion, and it is to that second aspect that we now turn. The notion that priests are called to represent Christ (in a strong sense: to make Christ present) strikes modern minds as curious and has needed considerable discussion. But the second aspect of the life of a priest – which is again representative – is much more straightforward. We began this discussion by noting that priests are Christians before they are priests, and as such, much of what they are called to be and to do is in common with all Christians. The Christian faith involves a commitment to prayer and the liturgy, to study in order to deepen knowledge of the Scriptures and the Christian tradition, to holiness of life, and to mission, whether you are lay or ordained. But here too there is something distinctive about the life of the priest. It is not that priests are 'first-class Christians' who must aim at a higher standard than everyone else, nor that we employ priests to be holy on our behalf, so that we need not bother. One standard applies to all, and that is perfection, the standard of Christ. But priests are a bit like advertising hoardings. Priests are called to live a Christian life in the public eye;

theirs is a Christian life writ large. This responsibility is partly a responsibility to the world, to show all people what it is to be a Christian (though the primary responsibility for this falls on the whole Church). It is much more a responsibility to the rest of the Church. By providing a public example of Christian life, priests stand as a reminder to their congregations of what it is to be a Christian, and so encourage them in the following of their vocation, in circumstances that may be much more difficult. It is not that every member of the congregation should strive somehow to become a crypto-priest. Rather, the obvious faithfulness of priests in their regular prayer, study and holy living should remind others of their call to continual prayer and to service of God and neighbour in ways that may be much less obvious. As was suggested in the first chapter, it is the particular vocation of the priest to make visible what it is to be a real person, the gift that Christ offers to all.

This second aspect of the life of a priest needs less discussion than the first because it is so much more familiar. It is not, however, without modern problems and confusions. Although we are still surrounded by other public figures, such as politicians and members of the royal family, and continue at least to some extent to expect them to be living examples of our moral values, these expectations are shifting. It is characteristic of such public figures that great scandal is caused by their failures to live up to the standards they represent. But the degree of such scandal has recently lessened, especially in the case of politicians, and some now question the whole idea of having such public figures. Is it fair to the individuals concerned? But priests continue to have this responsibility – a responsibility chosen and accepted at ordination – to present to their congregations a public example of the Christian life to which all are called; and they still cause great offence when they neglect this, whether by an immoral life or by carelessness in their prayers, liturgy and study.

The acceptance of this responsibility does not imply that the priest must achieve immediate perfection. It does require a continual striving after perfection, by God's grace (persistence in this despite and through failure can indeed be a powerful example). This second aspect of the priestly life is as deeply embedded in the tradition as the first. It lies for instance behind the requirement of the Church of England, following long tradition, that all its priests should say the office – Morning and Evening Prayer – daily in church. And it is given explicit expression in the Exhortation in the Ordering of Priests in the Book of Common Prayer: 'We have good hope ... that ye may so endeavour yourselves from time to time to sanctify the lives of you and yours, and to fashion them after the rule and doctrine of Christ, that ye may be wholesome and godly patterns and examples for the people to follow.' But the continuation of this aspect of priestly life amid the changes in modern Church and society need not be problematic, at least not in the way in which the other aspect is. Christ's own example of what it is to live as a true person in dependence on the Father is not gender-specific; it lies open to all, women and men. This in turn suggests that both men and women can provide a pattern of Christian life, a poster, an advertisement, that is consonant with tradition and up to date, and can have something to say to all. It would be fair to add that providing a better balance in the provision of such public Christian lives has been one of the most widespread arguments in favour of women's ordination.

The unity of priestly life

These, then, are the two basic aspects of priestly life: the making present of Christ to his people; and the public representation of the primary characteristics of the Christian life, of something of what it is to be a 'real person'. This ministry is priestly in both its aspects because both make present to the people of God the reconciling work of Christ, just as did the New Testament ministries that lie at its foundations. Both aspects involve the performance of specific tasks (such as the celebration of the sacraments and the praying of the office) and more general responsibilities (such as pastoral care, or study), but neither can be reduced to a list of things to be done. Both involve the whole person, offered in a complete life, lived so as to become one particular likeness of Christ. One thing that binds these two aspects of the priestly life closely together has already been noted: both these aspects of priesthood are lived within the body of Christ and for the sake of that body. They are indeed gifts given by God, that belong to the whole body; received for the body by certain members, they help the whole body fulfil its vocation to be sacrament (a place where Christ is truly present) and each member of it to become the person they really are, to attain (as the Prayer Book Ordinal puts it) the 'ripeness and perfectness of age in Christ'. Something of this is captured by the modern term 'collaborative ministry', which points to the Church as the place where each person, including the priest, uses their particular gifts for the service of all. (This is what the Christian understanding of working together [Latin *collaborare*, to work together] should be – in contrast to the unscriptural idea that in the Church, everybody should do everything, an idea with which collaborative ministry has sometimes been confused.) But apart from the fact that the two aspects of priesthood both exist for the sake of the whole Church, there are other things that unify the priestly life, and two in particular deserve to be mentioned.

The first is bound up with the conception of the priest as growing in a particular way into the likeness of Christ, an idea that has been central to this chapter. It is evident enough that the first two aspects of priesthood that we have identified will involve priests in living in the image of Christ. How else could they hope to make him present to their congregations? But the second aspect is equally Christlike, for if Christ is the revelation of what it is to live a perfect human life in loving obedience to God, priests, in attempting to offer a public example of Christian life, will again be living in Christ's image. Both aspects of priestly life are in the image of Christ and are lived in dependence on him. Furthermore, the relation of the two aspects of the priestly life – standing before the people in the name of Christ and as a public representative of what the whole people is called to be – have at least an analogue in the person of Christ. As both God and man, Christ revealed both the nature of God to humanity and the true nature of humanity to itself.

The second point really flows from the first. To some it will seem scandalous that so little has been said of the Eucharist in this chapter on priesthood, other than to note that the celebration of the sacraments is an important part of a priest's life. But to start a discussion of priesthood by describing the priest as the president at the Eucharist is to risk seeming arbitrary. Why should the priest preside at the Eucharist? At the start of a discussion of priesthood, this may well seem unclear; but at this stage of the discussion, it should become evident. In their lives, priests seek to follow the pattern of Christ, so that his work of bringing God to humanity and humanity to God can go forward. And it is at the Eucharist that these two aspects of the priestly life, and their relation to Christ and to the whole body of the Church, come together. At the Eucharist the priest stands as the public representative of the people, doing obviously what it belongs to all to do, that is, joining with Christ in his self-offering to the Father and responding to the gift of Christ with praise and thanksgiving. The priest is also there as a living sign of Christ, doing what he did and so by this *anamnesis* (making memorial) enabling his presence to be real to all. In both these things, the priest is acting in dependence on Christ, and in and for the sake of the whole body of Christ, which is there brought into unity. So at the Eucharist, and in the priest's presidency of the Eucharist, the two aspects of priestly life, which should characterize all that a priest is and does, are fused, and shown to exist not in isolation, nor for themselves, but in and for the whole people of God.

Priesthood today – and always

It is the purpose of this book, reiterated at the beginning of this chapter, to provide a model of priesthood and of priestly formation *today*. It may now be objected that this chapter has proceeded almost without reference to the particular conditions of priestly ministry in modern Britain (with the exception of references to the ordination of women, and to MSEs), and so can hardly expect to succeed in its aim. But this is to miss the point. As has been clearly stated in the discussion, the experiences of priests and the demands put upon them will change from place to place and age to age. Priests in Britain today are not identical to their Victorian counterparts, still less to George Herbert or to the priests of the early Church. But what this discussion has sought to do is to display those essential characteristics of priesthood – its relation to Christ and its place in the Church – which will be found in any priesthood, even in the most sharply differing circumstances. The challenge for each age is to discover how in those particular circumstances priesthood can flourish, as a vocation to live so as to make Christ present to his people, and so as to offer a public example of the Christian calling. If priesthood is less than this – if it is no more than an example, or is reduced to a set of jobs that anyone can do, and cease to do, or if it becomes an excuse for the creation of a self-centred coterie – then the whole body of Christ will suffer. It is therefore crucial that formation for the priesthood is of a sort that will enable this ministry to flourish for the sake of all; and it is to the proper nature of such formation that we turn in Part Two.

Note

1.   For very good reasons there is a growing tendency today to prefer the term 'presbyter' to the word 'priest'. For our purposes, however, it has seemed better to use the word 'priest' almost exclusively. The problem is not with the use of 'presbyter' but with the fact that there is more than one way of understanding it. If it is to be favoured, it needs to be able to assume the kind of theology we outline in this book; it could also cause confusion for some readers unfamiliar with its use. The word 'priest' is the term used in the Anglican ordinals, and the studied avoidance of it in recent discussion of ministry is potentially misleading. In the long run, whether 'priest' or 'presbyter' becomes the generally favoured word, we still need to rediscover the roots of the language and its use in the Anglican tradition, as well as in the wider Church.

PART
TWO

CHAPTER FOUR

Types of knowing

'He's hopeless – we do with him what we can, but he's never going to be up to much. With a family like that, there's very little hope of doing anything with him.' John Chipps sipped his hot tea gingerly, and picked up a biscuit.

'I have never been able to work out the make-up of that family,' said Alison. 'I've called on them because of my involvement with the youth group, but if there's anybody ever at home it only seems to be the children.'

John Chipps asked the secretary to bring Andrew's file. 'Their Dad went off two or three years ago,' he said, fishing out a bunch of school reports, 'and Mrs Jackson seems to have a full-time job plus work in the evenings. That's how she keeps them fed and well dressed. She's quite an impressive woman in her own way, but there's not much home life. If you're black in an area like this you're already at a disadvantage, as you well know, but if you lack so many of the things that most of the other kids take for granted, then you're doubly sensitive, and doubly angry. You see,' he said, skimming through the reports, 'he is a bright lad, but with hardly any ability to concentrate or get down to his work. Consistently poor marks, not through inability but through sheer failure to apply himself. He'll never do any good, I'm afraid.'

Alison walked off down the school drive deep in thought. 'But do they really know him?' she thought. 'He's a different boy at the youth club.' The lad was in big trouble at school for continuous misbehaviour and now for threatening a shy lad with a knife. True, it was a butter knife, but it seemed to bode ill for the future. John had called Alison into his office after her lesson to have a word about it; but Andrew himself didn't seem to her so much delinquent as lacking in common sense – immature and silly. What does it take to know a person? Can school teachers really know their pupils? Can a mother truly know her son? They all think they know. They see enough of the person, they see what they see. But often we only see the other one's response to us, not the whole person as they really are, and as they are in other settings.

It was to give Alison a secret pleasure in the next few years to see Andrew pass his GCSEs with high marks for the work he had put in, and off his own bat to apply for university and be offered two places. Eventually many years later, and not without a string of vicissitudes, he was to be a leading light in the theatre. And all the better at it for having done it in the teeth of misunderstanding from those who thought they understood him.

The place where he had been able to put down some roots which were the salvation of him was the youth club and then the church. Years later he once said to Alison, 'You know, I often think we are bad, bad, bad at understanding each other; and yet many Christians seem so damn sure they know God, and what he wants. And all the time they're making even more of a mess of him than they did of me. It's the difference between knowing somebody and just knowing a few bits and pieces about them. Many Christians today wouldn't allow God to ask them to love him.'

We have been tracing some of the roots of Christian priesthood. Among these roots lie three questions. 'Who are we?' came first, and here we found ourselves faced not so much with ourselves as with the person of Christ, addressing us and calling us. That led us in the next chapter to examine how we belong together, and yet again we found the person of Christ, this time in the physical sacrament of the Church, which continues in our midst the mystery of the incarnation. Only then were we able to ask '*Who* is the priest?'.

Becoming what we are

Becoming a person is not something that can be worked at in the way that we work at learning to drive a car or to type. Becoming a person happens through relating to others; it happens through the sacraments and the life of the Church; and all of this is in reality a mutual exchange with God, the receiving of gifts at his hands. The priest is clearly a person. To be a priest is not simply to have something added on but rather to become a priest through and through. (That is, if you like, a person who is wholly a priest, and a priest who is wholly a person.) We have spoken above of the distinctiveness of the priest. We have resisted much in the contemporary tendency to underline how the priesthood is like any other caring profession. And yet we have spoken of distinctiveness not as something which elevates the priest, or that suggests an individual possessing special powers. Rather is it the Church which gives us the basis for talk about the priesthood as distinctive – the making present of Christ to his people and the public representation of the primary characteristics of the Christian life.

In addition to that, our examination of the mystery of human life has led us to say that a priest is made by God. None of us 'makes' himself or herself; indeed the way we traditionally speak of a 'vocation to the priesthood' underlines the persistent belief that a person becomes a priest *in response* to the call of God. And this call is not a single message on a Friday afternoon in August, as it were, but an enduring address of God to us, throughout our whole life. All of this has implications for the ways in which the Church will foster vocations and assist their development.

It is now time to look more closely at the life of the priest, this time from another perspective, that of how the priest is trained. When people are trained for ordination they are introduced to some aspects of their future ministry in much more concentrated form. A good deal of light can therefore be thrown on our picture of the priesthood by looking at it through the lens of ordination training.

Education?

Before we proceed to do this in the following chapters, a clarification needs to be made. In the contemporary Church of England preparation for ordination is frequently referred to as 'theological education'. It is assessed almost exclusively by educational criteria, and the whole process is spoken of as one of *education*. No one doubts that education is necessary, nor that high academic standards are vital in both teaching and attainment. But a vocabulary and practice that amount to no more than education fail to leave us properly attentive before the God who calls and creates us. We have the same problem with our use of the word 'theology'. This is taken to mean theological study. Candidates for the priesthood are often described first and foremost as 'doing theology'.

It is instructive to compare these presuppositions with other walks of life. Someone training to be a footballer, for instance, can hardly be spoken of as being educated in football, for football involves the whole person, intelligence, emotions, muscle, and the skill which is born from inspired use of them all in concert. Or could the training of nurses be described primarily as 'medical education'? Such a change in approach could create alarm in the general public. Or we could take the police. If training of the police came to be spoken of as 'education in enforcement of the law', it would seem apparent to many that essential dimensions of this sensitive role were missing. In fact, in a wide variety of vocational fields, be they the caring professions, the arts, the crafts, or commerce, you can say that if the primary emphasis is on education or on an '-ology' alone, then something has gone wrong.

'Training' is another possible word, and we sometimes use it here for the sake of clarity. However, it lacks some of the important connotations of the word 'education' (and is also the word used for making dogs jump through hoops). Better still is 'formation'. The Latin *forma* means both outward shape and inner nature. Formation suggests something that affects the whole person, not merely the brain. Some might recoil from this: does it not suggest taking a group of people in all their variety and individuality and putting them through a machine turning out identical sausages? We are helped here by a third meaning of the Latin *forma*: the beauty of a person. True formation is a process whereby the unique beauty of each person is drawn out, the beauty of the 'image' of God in them. If they are called to be priests, then that is the form that will emerge, each one truly individual and full of their own particular life, but also growing up into that distinctive charge which God is putting upon (or calling forth from) them.

In the following pages we look at the life of the priest; and we examine it partly through the 'lens' of ordination training. In the process we shall see that just as the training involves not simply education but formation of the whole person, so also the priest's lifelong ministry involves not merely skills, but gifts, and not just personal effort, but much more a waiting on God's enduring call.

CHAPTER FIVE

Till Christ be formed in you

The saga of Beverley's baby would not go away. The problem was that her husband Wayne suspected it wasn't his baby. There was a dispute as to whether it looked like him. Kath said it did, but Wayne's mother claimed it didn't. Tony didn't know about this complication, and naturally couldn't understand why his refusal to do the baptism met with such vehemence. Unknown to him, it cast further doubt on the baby, whatever reasons he might give. In the end Kath resorted to the curate as an ear for things that couldn't be said to the vicar.

Tony's face went white when Kevin told him. 'Lord,' he said, dumbfounded. 'How do we get out of this one?' The parish's carefully-established baptism policy would collapse if he gave way. Tony couldn't get it off his mind. 'What the hell can we do?' he thought in sleepless hours in the night.

A few days later the deanery chapter met. Reg Keen, who had a parish without a church on a housing estate, was giving a talk on the presence of God in daily life. 'When will we learn,' he said, 'that God isn't imprisoned in a church building, and isn't a monopoly of our holy huddles. He is out there, where the real life is. We have got to learn from people where they are about where God is. He's interested in them, not in our churchy goings-on. You've only got to look into people's faces to recognize God.'

'You've got to be joking!' thought Tony to himself. 'If only it were so simple!'

Now it happened that the vicar of Beverley's parish was Reg. There was no church, and hence Beverley's fight to have the baptism at St Peter's. Reg was very good at visiting, and that very evening who should he call on but Beverley and Wayne? He didn't get a very warm reception.

'Church people are all hypocrites,' said Wayne. 'They sit there in smug satisfaction in their posh buildings, and don't do anything for anybody.'

'But God isn't imprisoned in churches,' said Reg, 'it's about life as it really is. All of life is holy.'

'What about God, then?' asked Wayne.

'Wayne ... ' pleaded Beverley, dreading what this might lead to.

But Wayne was just getting going. 'It's all fairy stories, innit?'

'God is real,' said Reg, undeterred. 'He's in everything. We meet him in each other. Why, it's just like your baby over there – just as you can see your face in his, we can see God in each other.'

Wayne looked at him with disbelief, and then he exploded: 'Just take a look at the bleeder and you tell me!'

Now Reg was not a very resourceful man, but after an instant's blind terror in which the awful truth dawned on him, he had an inspiration which he often remembered in later life with gratitude. He looked up at the quivering Wayne. 'Show me a photograph of you as a baby.' Now this was unexpected. Poor Beverley rooted in a box in a cupboard and miraculously found one. 'There. Now look at that.'

They all stood round the pram and looked from the baby to the photograph and back again. It could have been the same baby. The same strange twist to the mouth, the same elongated head.

Reg was there late into the night. Apology, forgiveness and reconciliation were but a part of it. Wayne was monumentally relieved to have been given a way out of a corner. It had started as innocent teasing but quickly got out of hand when Beverley teased back and was taken seriously. It became such that he couldn't retreat, and they had both sulked. Now Reg had come along and provided an objective solution. Reg insisted on baptizing little William, and he was duly done in the school hall on a Sunday morning.

The incident sowed a doubt in Reg's mind. How could we

recognize the unseen God in each other, if we were hopeless at recognizing those whom we had seen? He found a desire to see God, to feel after him and find him. This was no dramatic conversion – he was the same old Reg. He still resisted putting up a church. But there was something new nagging at him now: the vision of God, and how it might be found. Beverley and Wayne, with William in tow, became regulars: living, weekly reminders of a dimension which perhaps he had to take more seriously. Tony got him interested in icons, and it wasn't long before he was saying the daily office. Yet Reg never thought of the incident as a religious experience. It was more a question of expanded horizons.

Christ walks through Galilee looking for those who have it in them to be messengers of the kingdom and builders-up of a new community. The response of the disciples wells up from their unconscious, they are taken over by things they cannot comprehend and are incapable of analysing. They are riveted by a commanding presence, by a person who fills up all their inadequacies, who proceeds notwithstanding, dismissing all their slip-ups, and pointing them with confidence to awesome things they would never have dreamt of aspiring to, were it not that he never took 'no' for an answer.

For the disciples and all who were drawn to Jesus it was the nature of his personality that decided it – in him they saw someone who was more *a person* than they were. In him they saw that being a person was something much larger than they had realized. When the apostles took the good news to the four corners of the earth, they did it in response to a person. In him they had seen what it is to be human, and had become infected by it. They had put off their old humanity and Christ was putting on them a new one.

This transforming encounter with its dramatic results was not an experience unique to the disciples: through the centuries it has continued – the person of Christ is the content of his call. The body of Christ is galvanized not by knowledge alone, nor teaching, nor conviction, but the presence of One who expands the horizons of what it is to be a person.

The incarnation is the first sacrament. It was not then

withdrawn again, reducing us once more to 'spiritual' and 'personal' avenues – on the contrary, God inaugurated a new mode of sustaining physical contact, in the form of his body the Church. Paul proclaimed that we are the body of Christ, the sacrament of his continuing presence. This can already be seen on the road to Emmaus, where they knew him in the breaking of the bread, and in Paul's own eucharistic theology, where the sharing of bread and cup show forth the Lord's *Pascha*. (Pascha is the word for both passover and Easter – it refers to the event of passion, death and resurrection, and from it we get the English word 'paschal'.) In Paul's account of baptism similarly there is a real engagement in the water with the Lord in his dying and rising. Common prayer itself is a sacrament of the Lord's presence, for 'Where two or three are gathered together in my name, there am I in the midst of them'. All of these are reasons why, until very recently, worship was seen to be our Galilee, the place where we are galvanized by this frontier-stretching person. Worship until recently has stood at the very centre of the Christian life. It is the focus where we are brought to that transforming encounter with Christ which once turned the disciples into apostles.

Many people still think that worship is at the centre of the Christian life, but the way that worship is treated often shows this not to be the case. In the training of deacons and priests today worship often appears a secondary matter, and when the same people are later at work in the parishes the widespread collapse in the cultivation ('cult') of Christ becomes all too apparent. Many clergy either do not pray, or conduct prayer in a trivial manner, or simply find it very difficult to sustain. Many do not seem to realize what a poor state their prayer is in. Perhaps nowhere more than here is future ministry closely dependent on initial training. Certain important aspects of that training stand out, and they not only reveal to us how candidates for ordination should be prepared, but also show us major priorities in the whole priest's life.

All for God

Only a person with the thickest, dirtiest spectacles could peruse the Scriptures and find there a God who wanted to direct all attention away from himself and towards the service of others.

Only such a person could find there a people too, whether Jewish or Christian, which was not profoundly religious in the most religious sense: in the passionate cultivation of God. The Ten Commandments call for a love of God which occupies all our faculties; the prophets, whatever their message, all start with the sovereignty of God; and as for the psalms, the bulk of them express 'the soul's fundamental search for God in all its moods and phases of triumph and depression, in all its exultant joy and its profound misery ... it is to this religious consciousness, thus brought to full and conscious expression, that the revelation of Christ appeals.' Thus spoke the Christian socialist Charles Gore, who lived in an age when people still had the capacity for 'religion', the direct cultivation of God.[1] The Israel of the Old Testament is riveted by the transcendent God. In the New, Christ leads us to a new dimension of the same experience, through his relationship with the Father. In Christ we see a model of that direct prayer to 'Abba' which was so vital that Jesus had at times to get away from people, whatever their needs, in order to be faithful to it. Then with Paul we see a 'religious' homing-in of the greatest passion towards God. Everything is so much rubbish by comparison. His is a life lived all for God. In the Book of Revelation this sovereign faithfulness to God is so awesome that it can seem pitiless towards the millions of creatures who fail him, were we not aware of the dramatic conventions of the apocalyptic style. In all of this there is love of neighbour, yes, and there is indeed social consciousness, and there is selfless service and all those things which we prize so highly today. But it is all within a much larger frame than we can easily comprehend in our comfortable society: God himself.

The modern obsession with our neighbour can be seen as an inevitable reaction after a disastrous retreat by the Church in recent centuries into a churchy holy of holies. The reaction has been massive and without precedent. It is without precedent even in the New Testament. Many modern Christians would find their New Testament counterparts unbearably religious. The situation was perhaps inevitable, and something needed to happen, but we are often unaware of the extent to which we are gripped by reaction rather than balance.

Theology (as it is widely understood today) is taught, but God is caught. If we are to be opened up to that which is 'caught, not taught', and if this is going to be possible in local Christian communities, then it has to be found first in the training of the clergy, so that it will be the rock on which they are founded all their life through. Worship is the well of life for all Christian living. If we do not worship, we have nothing to believe in and nothing to say about God, and then our theology is useless. Karl Rahner takes to task 'the view that that which constitutes the true essence of Christianity, the true heart and centre which alone is signified in all its doctrines, the true task of the Church, consists in something which can simply be called "love of neighbour" or ... "commitment at the level of social politics and criticism of society", "responsibility for the world"'. This he calls pure 'horizontalism', and says that it constitutes 'that which, in the traditional terminology, should be called apostasy'.[2] If there is no direct relating to God, there can be no talking about him.

Our *theo-logy* arises out of an encounter with *Theos* (which is Greek for 'God'). It is just the same with human beings: our opinions about them depend on our having met them. I would not value your opinion of Gertie Throckmorton if you had never met her. How can we have ideas about God if we do not seek to encounter him? The liturgy has to be at the heart of all formation of Christian priests, and in such a way that it becomes in a natural and unselfconscious way the life-blood of all the teaching and life together in the formation-community. It is not enough merely to have a good sense of community, to which worship is attached. There has to be a real marriage of community and worship, so that the liturgy *is* us. Lancelot Andrewes said of the liturgy in one of his sermons that, 'being much in it, we shall even turn into it'.

Fervour

Such an attitude can only arise out of a strong piety. This word has somewhat negative connotations in English, but there is no other word near enough to what we want to say. In its best sense it is that kind of seriousness, commitment and love of God and of the things of God which can be mirrored in our reverence for a great work of art, or for people who are going through tremendous suffering, or love for our family and children. It is both commitment and being caught-up, and it accords such integrity to its object that it delights in anything which can be done for its good. Fervour or piety in this sense is love between two persons which is as great as, and yet greater than, any human love. The one person in this relationship is God, and the other is the human individual, and also in another sense the body of Christ, the Church. In an isolated compartment piety turns sickly: it is like many substances (like salt or iron) which are vital to our health, but in exaggerated quantities become poison. When it is entirely absent, however, the whole body ails. When we speak of piety and fervour this is what we mean – a seriousness about the quest for God which needs to be there in stronger doses in the mix of modern Christian life: which needs in fact to be rediscovered.

If a strong piety will naturally put the liturgy at the centre of the community's life, what are the signs that confirm this to be the case? There are some obvious ones: the time that is given to worship and prayer in the timetable, a place of worship which is treated with the same care as our own home, the care with which worship is prepared, its style, music and presentation, and the degree to which it is a part of the very fibre of the community's life. Worship lived in this way has other effects which are more difficult to put our finger on. The courtesy of reverent daily worship has an inevitable effect on the courtesy and care with which we live with others. It also has a profound effect on our study of the faith. This can come home very clearly to anyone who like the present writer has the experience of teaching liturgy in a theological college and also in a university. The university teaching is likely to be more self-conscious and taxing, because the subject is not being swum in daily, by all the participants together in community, and so it is hard work enabling it to be more than a fish on a slab. The students may be marvellous, but they are not being formed for the ministry, and therefore inevitably will start at a disadvantage in a subject such as this, when compared with those who are experiencing it several times a day in community (whether in a college or in a parish).

Students and staff in ordination training will need to ask themselves: 'What do we revere?' The answer will reveal much. In the most basic terms, we can say that a healthy reverence will be two-pronged, both horizontal and vertical: for God in our neighbour and for God in the Church-at-worship. Christianity has always had problems with exaggerated reverence: either for the Church and her worship, or for the 'world'. Either of these exaggerations can lead to sentimentality (sugary religion or diminishing of our neighbours by idealizing them) or to legitimation of ideologies (such as the Inquisition on the one hand or a totally social gospel on the other). But without God we are nothing, while to seek him with fervour and to feel the touch of him is to be clay taken up by fire, or, as George Herbert puts it in his poem 'Aaron', it is to live within another music:

> Only another head
> I have, another heart and breast,
> Another music, making live, not dead.
> Without whom I could have no rest:
> In him I am well dressed.
>
> Christ is my only head,
> My alone-only heart and breast,
> My only music . . .

John Robinson and many others made great use in the 1960s of the phrase 'ultimate concern'. If that phrase can be applied both to our neighbour and to the liturgy, without over-idealizing either, then perhaps we may then be preparing priests to follow in the steps of the apostles.

The given-ness of the liturgy

Many things in life make strong demands upon us. In Christian history worship has belonged among these things. Just as family life demands a pattern of being together at home rather than individual drifters-in and -out of a house, so too does worship. Whenever we gladly take on obligations, they become simply 'there', they come to have a given-ness which is larger than our momentary needs, urges, feelings, inspirations. In the same way, worship is there because it is there, and we are glad it is so, even if sometimes it goes against the grain.

This quality is a function of community. In theological colleges and training courses for ordination it is one way of describing how worship should be at the centre of the life. It is simply there. If you go to Margate for a holiday, well, the sea is simply there. If you become a Christian, prayer to God and public worship are simply there. If you have the charge of priesthood laid upon you, then the Sunday liturgy, the daily office and private prayer are simply there, and there is no way around them, even should you want one. They are part of the bargain, and they grow on us as we increasingly sense in them something of the sovereignty of God. In this way they become both a commitment and a joy, even if there are times when we would rather be doing something else.

The 'there-ness' is not a matter of law or rules, but a part of the essence of being Christian. We are not being constrained by rules, but taking on what we have embraced with our eyes open, knowing that it is filled with promise, and the one who makes the promise is faithful. When people are being trained for the priesthood, whether in a resident community or on a course during which they live at home and sustain a job, something has to be done to enable the given-ness of the liturgy to come home with a monumental force. In a resident community this is easier. For a non-resident course student in a parish this exposure should ideally centre on the parish worship. In an imperfect world this presents difficulties, but it is so central to what formation is about that it is vital that it be there with all its weight.

The form of liturgy that is used and the way it is done are of course important considerations, but only to a certain extent. Experiments in clergy training with using different forms of office and Eucharist and different patterns of daily life may well give the students an opportunity for a little liturgical supermarket-strolling: what it will not introduce them to is the relentlessness of the real thing in the parish (or in any Christian community). Not only is this a case of 'forewarned is fore-armed': the relentlessness is part of the essence of what the whole thing is about. It is concerned with the constancy of years rather than a life of 'pick and mix', which is never sustainable.

Finally, the liturgy is a rhythmic animal, and its rhythms are as close and relentless as music. Teaching timetables have to fit round it, and not vice versa (even if this wreaks havoc with travel, mealtimes, etc.). This is the real measure of its 'is-ness' – it simply cannot be dropped to make way for other things. To do such a thing is like deciding not to turn up at home one night. It has to be unthinkable. Once it is in principle unthinkable then it can be open to small adjustments in grave necessity. In the parish it is the same. Weekday services have to go on – the gathered faithful cannot be left in the lurch. And where the daily office is established in the right way the congregation will happily get on with it if the vicar is detained for one reason or another.

The imagination

Having established that as the rock on which we build, we then need to look at how it is possible for leaders of Christian congregations to exercise their imagination in worship. This is done at the routine level by constant sensitivity to the others present. This needs the utmost lightness of touch, but involves the ability to imagine ourselves in our neighbours' shoes, to be aware of where the liturgical going is tough for them, of where they are failing to understand, where they are being excluded, and all the varied dynamics of a worshipping group. Such an attitude could be oppressive or fussy, and can wreck worship through too many announcements of pages or other manifestations of the obtrusive clerical compère. It needs great lightness of touch. Prospective clergy also need not to shout or rush in church, not to lead commonly recited prayers with a loud voice, and not to develop habits of panic or nervous mannerisms. Those and many other such things often only require a little more imagination.

Imagination is also needed at the planning stage. Are services simply to run their course, or are people to work together now and again to produce something fresh and lively? (We pray for lightness of touch here too.) The given-ness of worship is like the tree, but the Christian liturgy is both tree and the ecosystem of the Spirit. It is a 'grid' through which passes the sap of the Church; but it is also life abundant which cannot be pinned down, inspired as it is by the Holy Spirit who blows where he wills. The living world of the liturgy is the other side of the coin of 'given-ness': the given-ness of human beings, and the compelling voice of their own vivid experience. This 'life within the tree' is our desire to evaluate, our desire to give, to create, and to make the liturgy our very own, rather than glumly accepting hand-ons.

The living plant of the 'authorized' liturgy engages with the 'life' of our personal and corporate experience. This relationship, however, is fraught with difficulties. There is a tension which can never be escaped, and there is also a natural tendency for the 'tree-ness' of the liturgy to gain the upper hand and kill everything. Then pent-up tension leads to explosion. So the medieval liturgy became a tangled, suffocating bush. The reaction of the Reformation was towards greater freedom. However, the tree was badly damaged in the process, impairing the very search for life more abundant. The eighteenth-century Book of Common Prayer liturgy brought a similar explosion in the Oxford Movement. The Tridentine Roman liturgy burst apart in a ferocious reaction which left many stunned, as the Second Vatican Council produced its radical liturgical reforms. It is dangerous to be unaware of the stultifying powers of the tree, and dangerous also to be unaware of the extent to which our cherished ideals are exaggerated reactions.

On the other hand, the 'life' of the tree-world when left to itself (such as in revival movements) can bring vitality and seem to make living connections between worship and experience, but in the long run it always collapses inwardly through lack of a life-support system. Our problem is like balancing a broom on our nose: how to co-operate with God so that 'tree' and 'life' stay in the relationship which he wills for them. We tend to see something like the ASB as *being* the liturgy: but a mere book can never provide all that is necessary.

> ...if an architect were to draw up plans for a house suitable for any family on earth, ... [he should] not be surprised if ... the house did not suit every family ... When we know that a house has three floors, with a living room and kitchen on the ground floor, bedrooms on the first floor and an attic at the top ... and that it has tables, beds and chairs, ... this does not tell us whether a particular family will like the house, enjoy living in it and feel at home ... [So with the liturgy, a] prefabricated house has to be made habitable.[3]

We need to be exact and discerning in our interpretation of this. We are speaking not of a compromise between tree and ecosystem, or of a truce, or of a trade-off, but of a real unity, in which the monumental 'there-ness' of the liturgy is truly lived in an imaginative way within the real constraints of real life. It is a great help if a community (be it college, parish, or something else) worships regularly in a public or semi-public building. In a parish this is not a problem, but it becomes a problem in colleges and on courses for at least two reasons. First of all, a private chapel where a college can have free rein may have the advantage of allowing people to gain varied experience, but it will not expose them to the essentially public nature of the liturgy. 'Designer' worship varying from day to day in a private chapel, meeting people's desires for the 'meaningful' and intimate, is inculcating illusions which cannot be satisfied in real life. It is an irony that the worship of many groups which lay a great emphasis on the secular Christ turns out to have this quality of the 'holy huddle'. Worship in a small chapel can be good for very small groups in a parish, but for a corporate body the size of a college, a worship area which is a close fit can emphasize still further the sense of being turned inward. The community needs to expand into a large building which requires us to sense beyond ourselves, and doesn't hug our contours like a glove, but has an independence of its own. Even when, as is usual, worship is in a small private chapel, these things should be borne in mind.

Secondly, this kind of 'holy huddle' worship which can be found with colleges and courses is the fruit of a clearly-defined group, something which can never be said of a parish congregation. There needs to be more of a sense of the Church – its variety makes it more intractable, but its true greatness enables it all the same to rise above what may seem to be limitations. The greatness of it is God's greatness. Behind worship has to lie a serious ecclesiology (doctrine of the Church). It is because the Church is such serious business that the liturgy is serious business. It is not for ourselves but because of the body of Christ that we gather. Normal Christian worship cannot be compiled or composed for a group in isolation – it will be informed by the practice of the Church, and also by an adequate vision of the Church as sacrament. It is not *me* at prayer, it is not *us* at prayer, it is the Church at prayer, the voice of Christ in his Church.

There is a third way of exercising the imagination which is no less important than the other two. People who in preparation for ordination have been properly formed in the history and principles of the liturgy find that their apprehension of worship and what it is about is totally transformed, and through this they gain an interest which was not there before. This experience of the ordinand desperately needs to be the experience of all Christian people. A very urgent priority in the parishes is teaching about the liturgy, comparable to that which the clergy have received. This will need to impart something of the historical and technical detail of how the liturgy evolved. If something like this got off the ground it could profoundly affect the life of the Church.

Ascetical maturity

Worship is not there to provide experience, expertise, inspiration, or, indeed, anything. It is to be allowed to do in us whatever God wills to be done in and for us. This will bring surprises. These will include boredom, spiritual dereliction, breaking down of our pride and our will, as well as the nice things we want from it. It will be, among other things, a place of conflict, conflict at the presence of Christ. It will always be hard work. The Latin word *diligo* means 'I love', or 'I delight'. From it comes the word 'diligence'. One of the main ways in which love shows what it is worth is by its diligence. Collecting the spouse from the supermarket on time, helping with all the chores, and even something like changing the toilet roll when it runs out, rather than leaving it for someone else to do, that is love. Love (and liturgy) will demand a growth in diligence.

Worship in ministerial training will therefore need ascetical maturity in the teaching staff, and that same maturity will need to be fostered in the students. It follows without question that these qualities are essential in the parish priest. Such ascetical maturity comes out of demanding community life in which our corners are knocked off and we simply cannot get away with our individualism, self-obsession and wilfulness. It comes from submission to a regular life of worship and prayer and a formative experience which generates automatic cross-reference between academic study, common life with others, pastoral work, and prayer and worship.

Prayer needs to include a period each day set aside for being alone with God. There are many ways of approaching this, some of them open to question, such as listening to music or thinking all the time about ourselves and our life. All of those can have traces of prayer in them, but they are not the disciplined exercise of prayer. For that you need to read the right books and have a spiritual guide. However inadequate its providers may feel, spiritual guidance is essential in training for the priesthood and in the subsequent living of it. Students cannot be left to fend for themselves, and, if necessary, some of the teaching should go to make way for this guidance. Accumulation of much knowledge is useless if the spirit is not being nurtured, and if the Christian tradition on prayer is not being taken on board. Retreats are essential, and only worth doing if they are taken seriously. God needs to be given a chance, and, particularly in the maelstrom of the modern world, the silence of retreats needs to be as full as possible, with no escapes to the pub in the evenings. If we cannot face silence, that means we cannot face ourselves, and something is needing attention. The word 'spirituality' has its place, but is frequently misused and turned into a poodle. It needs treating with circumspection, and preferably used as little as possible. Talk of 'spirituality' often serves as an escape-hatch from the hard graft of getting to know the ascetical tradition.

Nothing less than apostles

The demands Jesus made on his disciples could be tough. But for the joy of what was held before them they accepted the discomforts and were prepared for the sacrifices. If being with Christ is a somewhat disconcerting experience, even more disconcerting must be the prospect of Christ being formed in us. It is no wonder that we seek all ways to avoid it. Yet if we truly have been designated by him and charged with taking up special service in the Church, then it would probably be best to turn and face him from the start.

Life together

Priests should be equipped to help their people in the life of the spirit, and also to be spiritual directors/companions to their fellow clergy. Much wisdom can be picked up by studying the classics, but there is grit in it which is basic, and is gained not by studying principles, but by having gone through a mill such as is provided by the demanding common life of a theological college. This basic stuff used to be a part of daily life in less affluent times, but now it is outside many people's experience. In a theological college in a country like Romania there is less need for close community because what it gives is found in ordinary

Christian living. But even in a country like Romania this is fast disappearing. In modern society the need is greater than ever for this kind of 'remedial treatment' as it might be called, which gives people a concentrated and demanding experience of community. Ways also have to be found for it to be passed on to the people in the parish; but what does such a common life mean, and how can it be introduced into parish life? That is the next question to demand our attention.

Notes

1. C.Gore, *The New Theology and the Old Religion*, London, 1907, pp.26f.
2. K.Rahner, *Theological Investigations* vol. 14, London: Darton, Longman & Todd, p.295.
3. J.Gelineau, *Liturgy Today and Tomorrow*, pp.14ff.

CHAPTER SIX

Life together

'Is this a house or a railway station? The only way I see the kids nowadays, John, is to stand in this kitchen and watch them pass through.' John and Ellen Chipps were seeing their teenagers start the flight from the nest in the precocious modern way.

'It's not our fault,' said John, 'it's the way all kids are – I reckon it's in the water supply.'

The next week it was Easter. 'You'd never believe it was the greatest day in the Church's year!' complained Tony. 'Half the pillars of the parish away on holiday – my best warden, John Chipps, in Tenerife, and the head server gone pony-trekking. No sense of letting the side down, never mind keeping Easter.'

Two weeks later, there was a deanery meeting. The East Botting team rector (Jim) and one of his team vicars (Ken) disagreed about the arrangements for a trip to Taizé. They had thought it was a team visit, but then Ken had decided to start organizing one of his own. Another vicar in the team muttered to his neighbour, 'We should never have had him – some bloomin' team! We didn't even meet the bloke until he'd been appointed. How do you call that a team?'

Mrs Pearson from the local theological college had come to speak, and was kept waiting through all this. She had to shorten her talk. Then during it some clergy started slipping out. Tony was just making for the door as she broke off and said, 'I don't think I shall accept another invitation to speak to a deanery – not only have you kept me waiting, but hardly anyone spoke to me over lunch, and now they're all slipping away. Do you have no sense of corporate responsibility and basic hospitality?'

Father Mark Smith was visiting Mrs Pearson's college as a diocesan director of ordinands. He almost missed supper as he got lost looking for the refectory, and afterwards found himself alone in his room. Going around looking for students, he found a few reading the newspapers. 'Do you know where I can find Mrs Pearson?'

'Oh, she should have gone home by now – she'll be back at nine in the morning.'

'Where does she live?' 'I'm not sure – I think it's about five miles away.' They went back to reading their papers.

Five students were sent to Tony's parish for a summer placement, but he had to send them away. They rejected the spartan accommodation in his vicarage, and refused to be available right through the day without having one third of it off. Such contractual attitudes made him see red, and he sent them packing.

The Bishop of Rumchester was fed up with the problems caused by Father Mark Smith. He was destroying the marvellous work of his predecessor through wilful decisions, and the parish was pretty fed up. The bishop was exasperated by so many clergy seeming unable to work either together or with their people. (He could hardly bear to think about the family front.)

The diocese of Rumchester was full of complaints. Not only was the bishop distant and inaccessible, but he took little interest in his clergy, and seemed more intent on turning the diocese into a well-run firm than on fostering community and the quest for God.

A group was meeting to discuss how parishes could encourage community life in their neighbourhoods. Tony, John Chipps, Mrs Pearson, Ken, Mark Smith and the Bishop of Rumchester had done quite a lot of reading and had now invited Sita, a Hindu woman, to speak to them. 'How to foster community?' she asked, and smiled. That was about as far as they got. The meeting proved to be very awkward. Tony thought afterwards that it sounded a bit like Kevin's meeting with the chief of the

Uduli. They could not succeed in finding the right question to ask, and he couldn't think why.

'Fragments, all is fragments. An unravelling of ancient threads, an incapacity to see what is being lost, habitual behaviour streaked through with fragmentation and irresponsibility. Will our children grow up like that too?' Sita asked her husband. The future seemed to her to promise an increasing fragmentation of family, of community, of courtesy and hospitality and of corporate responsibility. A fragmentation blind to its own poverty. 'The most tragic thing of all is that they think they can talk about it.'

———————

Like most teenagers I didn't particularly want to do the sort of things nor be the sort of person that my parents hoped and expected. University came as a great relief; at last I would have the freedom to be myself, to do what I wanted and not be limited by them nor the world in which I lived. This is a recognizable characteristic of teenagers, but one which I suspect stays with us in many forms throughout our lives. And it is, of course, very understandable. We all want to have a sense of ourselves and not be swept along by expectations and commitments and responsibilities which only seem either to serve the needs of others or to maintain the status quo.

We often feel then that other people get in the way of our being ourselves; they can stunt our growth, limit our potential and shackle our need for the space to discern 'who we are'. There is both a truth and an illusion in that. We do indeed attempt to manipulate and limit others, to take each other for granted and numb our sensitivity to the lives of those around us. But we are mistaken if we conclude from that that to 'be ourselves' (to be a person) involves somehow freeing ourselves from others and their needs, from being involved and caught up in relationship and commitment. Whatever the 'I' of ourselves is, it only makes sense, and it can only have identity *because* of others.

This 'identity-in-relationship' is in fact a reflection of the very nature of God, the God who is Trinity, for God is relationship and communication within himself. Each person of the Trinity exists, if you like, for the sake of the others, and each gains identity within the context of each other. Their identities are not blurred because of this, there is 'no confusion of persons'. There is no 'inner Christ' waiting to get out that is being overwhelmed by the Father. There is no essential 'Father' waiting to be actualized, if only he wasn't being frustrated by the Son. The Father is the Father because of the Son and vice versa. Or, in human terms, I am me and can only be me because of you.

The Church as the body of Christ is that human community which is grafted into this life of God. It is not simply a collection of individuals who have something in common, namely Jesus of Nazareth, nor is it simply a group of people who love and support one another – though hopefully it is at least that. Neither is it simply a 'boat from which to fish', i.e. a practical organisation which provides a basis for 'saving souls'. The Church is a mode of being, a way of relating and through it a way of perceiving and relating to the whole of creation. The Church is *koinonia*, it is communion.

As we have seen in the previous chapter of this book, being a priest is one way of being a person. Just as any individual can only find meaning within the context of others, so the person who is a priest only makes sense within the context of a community, the Church. Who and what a priest is comes from, and is lived out within, the life of that *koinonia*. That is why the 'common life' within priestly formation is to be seen as central, because it both points to and participates in that communion, for it is one in which the people who share it are all testing and discerning their vocation to priesthood and, through seminars to casual conversations over a cup of tea, what it means to be a priest is shaped, informed, questioned, enriched, criticized, deepened and glimpsed in that community.

The common life acts as a sort of cauldron in which all the other ingredients of formation, study, prayer, conversation, etc., are allowed to ferment and stew. It is not being suggested that at the end of two or three years' formal training the common life produces a self-contained package or a finished product, but rather that it allows those involved to taste and experience something of what the Christian gospel calls us to and to take that with us into the parish. Nor will it enable those who participate to 'escape' from the tensions and problems of the 'outside'; but on the contrary it will underline the fact that it is within the context of those tensions and problems that *koinonia* is located. Just as it is *with* the very stuff of creation, and not simply for it, that the incarnation is located, so a common life is concerned with the complexities of human living, and is not a retreat from or a seminar on them.

The grounding of such a life for those involved in ordination training will be the daily office and the Eucharist. The coming together of the staff and students at set times, regularly and consistently, to pray and worship together, marks the particularity of their common life. Of course it is not simply the explicit religious activities which bind people together, but the 'every-day-ness' of their life. Mutual responsibility, involving both staff and students, becomes extremely important. Others will depend on you to 'do your bit', whether that means making beds for guests, washing up after lunch, cleaning the chapel, or turning up on time for a music rehearsal. It also means learning, in contrast to our prevailing culture, that you are not in competition with those around you. There is no need to assert yourself over and against anybody else socially or academically, because the purpose is not to succeed at other people's expense. So for instance a student working on an essay which is proving to be difficult can seek help from fellow students as well as tutors, without any sense of cheating, because the essays mark growth in understanding and not simply a percentage of your overall mark. So it is that the changes and insights which communal living bring are brought about as much by your next door neighbour as your spiritual director, though in different ways.

Perhaps what underlines and runs through all of this is a blurring of the distinction between sacred and secular. We tend to polarize the spiritual and the physical, the transcendent and the immanent. The Church as *koinonia*, however, brings us continually back to the recognition that in Christ these are not competing opposites attempting to absorb one another, but elements joined in union so that all life becomes religious, and that communion extends not simply between persons but embraces all of creation.

Consequently a common life is not free, indeed cannot be free from the negative aspects of human living and the contradictions and tensions it brings. People will be stubborn, self-centred and downright childish. People will also become very vulnerable to comments and the attitudes of others; little things will become like mountains. They will lose sight of a greater vision and become embroiled in matters of detail. Despite being continually with others, people will also face times of loneliness, sometimes quite intensely (in the same way that you can feel alone at a party). The world in which you find yourself will feel alien and absurd and at times your own individuality and personhood will seem diminished; in other words all the usual aspects of human life, not least to be found in the parish, will be present. But the way you begin to respond and cope with that negative side will bear fruit when the person is ordained and working in a parish.

Common life, however, does provide the context in which connections can be made, even if only tenuous ones: connections between study and prayer, between casual conversations and the liturgy, between the needs of others and our own needs; connections which are very difficult to make in non-residence, where everything can seem to be compartmentalized. And this allows for growth and change as people are faced continually with others, and through others with themselves.

In other words such a model for priestly formation is not an escape from the 'real' world; it is not a game or a private club or a way of avoiding 'things that really matter' such as unemployment, the Third World or the homeless. For many, perhaps, the basic criticism of this model is exactly that: for our modern world, a common life seems to represent an anachronistic model of human living which is removed from reality, from the world as it is. It belongs to an age long past, to a world of scholarly monks and nuns, to holding on to a false security and illusory order when in fact such a world has been liberated by science, psychology, politics, sociology. To train and form people for priesthood surely should occur in the world and for the world. They should experience life in the parish, in the workplace, on income support, on the council estate, in the AIDS hospice – in the situations and places where the people they will minister to actually are.

There are two replies to that. Firstly, people who are living in community and training for the priesthood are not people without a past; they will represent a great variety of experiences and opinions, all of which will provide ingredients for the 'cauldron' in which everything is being 'stewed'. During training they will also be attached to parishes, become involved in organizations (I was a Samaritan for one year) and in the vacations will spend time in hospitals, more parishes, prisons or even abroad. In other words, a common life is not surrounded by a brick wall over which nothing comes in and nothing goes out. But again it provides the setting, the context, the space for reflection and the continual process of integrating responses to questions of personal identity, what it is to be a priest, what does it mean to pray, to understand the world in its complexity, etc.

Secondly and more fundamentally, to share a common life and to grow in what it is to be a priest through that life reflects the opening chapters of this book in which it was suggested that being 'a person' was essentially a gift from and through Jesus Christ, and that the person who is a priest is so, not because of qualifications or abilities, or because of the things they can do, but because of who they are within the context of what the Church is. Or, to put it another way, a priest is a certain sort of character within the whole story of the life of the Church.

An image like that one seems to be the opposite of what our society has come to treasure most – the stress on freedom, autonomy and choice as the essence of what it is to be human, to be a person. We attempt to find out who we are by abstracting ourselves from the particularity of situations, we search for meaning not in the context in which we are, but by withdrawing into ourselves and there hopefully find the resources by which we can choose, if not create purpose, meaning and identity. In a world which has become fragmented, where there seems to be not so much a lack of morality and interpretations of human identity, but on the contrary, so many of them, each competing, contradicting, asserting and counter-asserting, the only option is to find certainty and the answer to the questions 'Who am I?' and 'What shall I be?' within oneself. To engage in a common life is surely to surrender one's freedom, it is to allow one's individuality to be submerged and even overwhelmed by something else. It is inauthentic, escapist and unrealistic.

What seems to be the great strength of our modern world, its sense of freedom and individualism, bears, however the seeds of its own destruction, for the more we hold that our own opinions, beliefs and experiences are decisive, the more we assert ourselves over and against everything and everyone, the more we hold truth and meaning to be simply personal and a matter of choice then the more brittle and relative everything becomes. We are left living in what has been called a dialogue of the deaf. In our world in which certainty has been removed, we either decide that everything is relative, that nothing is important except personal integrity, security and wholeness, or we refuse to accept the plurality of society and become fundamentalists, staking our claim on the absolute authority of the Bible, or the Pope, or a particular brand of politics, etc. Either way there is no possibility of dialogue because there are no common reference points, no common framework in which dialogue can take place. It is perhaps no wonder that in the vacuum left by such fragmentation violence flourishes.

Many of the assumptions and processes which have formed our present understanding of what it is to be human and to be moral have had an equally strong effect on our religious convictions and on the Church itself. If everything is relative, if there can be no truth, then faith becomes a private affair and the Church is reduced to the functional. The gospel becomes a source of inner strength, particularly in times of suffering, and the Church becomes simply one among many other institutions which respond to the needs of society. The priest, even for the congregation, is seen as a symbol of what turns out to be a certain kind of bourgeois morality, centred around 'family values'. It is no wonder that on visiting a bereaved family, the priest is met with assurances that the departed might not have gone to church but that they did their best to help other people.

And so, increasingly unsure of what priesthood might mean in the modern world, and confronted with communities which are even more unsure, the parish priest is tempted to find relevance and a role in purely functional terms. The role becomes that of a professional Christian at the head of the congregation, a manager who must ensure the building is watertight and that the finances are sound, somebody who can try to raise the social conscience of the congregation and make them aware of the needs of those around them.

Yet behind all of this doing lies the suspicion that all seems to be of no avail. For every individual visited there are hundreds more still lonely. Every sermon preached is met with perhaps an occasional stirring of hope, but more likely with indifference and misunderstanding. And so our vision of God fades and the richness of Christianity is drained. Or perhaps it is because our vision of God, our grasp of the richness of Christianity, was not great enough. We had not tasted fully the givenness of the

Church; we had not immersed ourselves deeply enough into it.

As the common life shows us, the modern world has in a sense got it the wrong way around. We do not begin with ourselves, we do not have to construct meaning from nothing. It is already there in the ongoing life of the Christian community, in its *koinonia*. It is not a matter of one's own shaping but something which shapes us. If priests are indeed certain characters in the ongoing life of the Church then it is that story, that 'narrative' which will shape and form them. Priests cannot exist in a vacuum, nor can they make themselves. They will not be formed by following some courses in academic theology, managerial skills and communication techniques (important as they are). But they can be moulded by participation in and through the life of the Church, its *koinonia*.

What is more, it is only through their relationship with that life that they will be equipped to be priests for others. For only then will they be more than professional carers, managers, administrators, etc. Only when the lives of priests are grounded in the ongoing momentum of the Church do we see clearly that *koinonia* is not simply a theological concept, but is embodied in the Church, in the parish, in each and every baptized Christian. It does not matter that this may only be glimpsed and be very fragile, for it is enough to allow everything else to have meaning, from the priest desperately fumbling around for words that will comfort and heal those who are dying to making sure that the church building is indeed watertight. For we no longer have to feel threatened by the immensity of our task, nor by the sense that we are not completely free or in control of who and what we are, because the story goes on and the narrative, which is God's, continues.

So for priests as for all Christians, their personhood is formed and has its source in the community of the Church. The formal training of those to be ordained should not be located in abstract theories or courses in management or 'how to deal with people', but in the actual living out of that community, in the form of a common life. This, as we have suggested, is not simply a group of people who live together, essentially living their own lives. Indeed that has become one of the tragedies of our society. People live closed lives behind their locked front doors where once people actually knew their next-door neighbours. Even in halls of residence at universities where structurally some form of common life is in place, students can feel isolated, not knowing how to relate. Yet all have the possibility of being more than that of people simply doing their own thing, and it is for the priest to foster, in such situations, a richer, more human way of living. The home life of married ordinands, especially those on courses, is a source of what is being suggested here and can in itself illuminate and form what it is that a priest is about. It is all of this, residence at a theological college, married life, the couple of weeks those training on courses spend together (which should be seen as essential to their formation and not simply a holiday) which enables us to 'sniff out' the gifts which Christ freely offers and which can give a vision, even if it is one glimpsed in a darkened mirror, that is to be reflected in the parish.

Of course none of this can be an excuse for avoiding the continual questioning of the tradition of the Church and the never ending task of 're-earning' and 'repossessing' that tradition. The importance and significance of feminist theology, for example, cannot be ignored. Nor is it a licence for any kind of pastoral ministry and activity. And so we shall now go on to look at these in more detail.

CHAPTER SEVEN

Learning and the love of God

'Do you still want to start a revolution?'

'Well, Mr Hill, when I say that, I'm not silly enough to mean it.'

'Ah,' he wagged a spanner at her, 'but you did mean it. You're backing down now.'

'What I would like to do,' she said, 'is to succeed in teaching people, and seeing them really grow.'

'Do you mind telling me something, Alison?' he said. 'I admire your enthusiasm, it's a real tonic. What I want to ask is – can you tell me what fires you most?'

She thought a bit. 'The pastoral work fires me, the whole caboodle fires me – it's marvellous, even though it's always making you groan.'

He thoughtfully put away his kit. 'What part of it couldn't you do without?'

'The worship,' replied Alison. 'After all, it's the one place where the community is most like community. It feels most at home, doing what it was made for. But how did I get fired about it?' She realized to her surprise that it was the combination of the worship in her college with the lectures on liturgy. 'Both of them were very badly done. But it's still true, it was the *study* of worship which got me fired about it.'

'Why aren't I fired about it?' asked Mr Hill. 'And the rest of us in the pews – it would be nice to have something that you were on fire about. I know many people just want a quiet life – but still, it would be very good if you fired us, wouldn't it?'

Alison thought about this for a while and then said, 'What fires me must fire you. If clergy are grabbed by liturgy and people in the pew aren't, then the clergy have had an experience which the others haven't. Therefore,' she said, with one of the mannerisms of her mathematician husband, 'I must help people to have the same experience.'

The Lent course took the Eucharist as its theme, but instead of being chat-shops the groups were forced to work. They were to study the Last Supper and the origins of the Eucharist. Alison prepared the group leaders with formidable efficiency; together they prepared the printed material, and they set themselves the target of all participants being able to set out in simple form how the shape of the Last Supper is the shape of our Eucharist. The first week went well. The next week saw a few storm clouds on the horizon. In the third week the lid started to come off. Some couldn't remember from one week to the next what they had done. Some were shocked at the simplest critical approach to this most sacred story. Some got their facts so muddled that the four-action 'shape' became in their minds something like a board-game which the disciples played while they waited, or a loaf of bread twisted in a fourfold shape, or something akin to hand-jiving. One group dissolved in laughter when an old woman with an infectious and eccentric sense of humour sent the whole thing up. There were many misunderstandings. Sid Green thought that the curate was trying to tell them the holy Eucharist was just like eating fish and chips, and saw in this a threat to their Sunday service, for they had learnt about *agapes*, and had seen the picture of Maundy Thursday in Westminster Cathedral, when the Eucharist is celebrated at a long banqueting-table set the length of the nave.

All in all, the Lent course caused some confusion, a little turmoil, quite a lot of misunderstanding, and a lot of talk. On Maundy Thursday they set a table the length of the nave and turned the pews inwards. That did something. One or two stayed away, but for nearly all who came it eased them along a little in the direction in which Alison had hoped they would travel. The Gospel was re-scripted in the form of a play, acted by a small group, and naturally included the washing of the feet, but as part of the play. They marked the four actions by singing refrains. As the priest took the bread they sang 'He took the bread', and then they sang 'He took the wine' as the priest did just that. The eucharistic prayer was frequently interrupted with the refrain: 'He gave thanks', and as the priest did the fraction with the small loaves they sang, 'He broke the bread'. At communion the choir sang, 'He gave it to them – this is my body, this is my blood'.

The exercise had done everything to Alison – it had dispirited her, moved her, annoyed her, taxed her. There had been no revolution, but there was no doubt about it, an impression had been left on people. It was a start, and in a humble but significant way it had enabled everyone, including Alison, to taste together some of the fruits of study.

Study tends to be a Cinderella in the life of the parish clergy, and is one of the areas where with the best will in the world everything seems to militate against it. At their ordination, priests make a promise to 'be diligent . . . in all the studies that will deepen [their] faith and fit [them] to uphold the truth of the Gospel against error'. The primary aim of this study must be for deeper understanding of the faith which is to be lived out. It is not in order to be better pastors, to be more up to date in counselling, in psychology or in social criticism. These are of undoubted importance, but in themselves they are simply functional. The priest's study is about more than that.

Planning

Study needs time. It may mean planning courses or books a year in advance, possibly as part of a diocese's plan for regular review of ministry; there is a great deal to be said for seeking guidance on a planned scheme of reading. It will mean making time for study, and not treating it simply as something to fill in when a wedding is cancelled. It used to be the case that many priests reserved the morning for study and preparation of sermons, but for most people today this is neither practical nor congenial. In that case there is a lot to be said for the idea of fixing a whole day each month for study, and we should feel no reason for apologising for keeping such a day 'off-bounds'.

In choosing what to read, there is every reason to cast the net wide. Only to read commentaries on the Book of Joshua, or works on the 'big bang' theory would certainly lead to being well-read in those areas; but if we are to speak responsibly of God, then an openness to the world's challenges is also called for, to make possible an integration of wider aspects of experience and knowledge. If we are to speak responsibly of God, then there has to be care in planning what we read. It is important equally not to be indiscriminate in choice of study, but to base new areas for study on things either known or experienced.

The challenge of the other

There can be no doubt that this kind of study is something good in its own right in the priest's life. It is not, however, an isolated activity. Our desire for God, our desire to make God known and to pass on what we have received, arises from encounter with the one true person of Jesus Christ. We bring to our study the persons we are becoming as a result of our encounter with him. In more ways than one this is not simply study done by an individual: the way we learn, the changes our reading brings about in us, the difficulties we meet in the process, the challenges we encounter, are all part of the common life the priest shares not only with the Christian community, but also with fellow priests and deacons. If there is at its base an openness to the address of Christ, then we will grow in openness to those of different temperament, expression and belief. There is need for discussion of what we read with others, and this is something which can seem painfully absent in a priest's life.

Diversity in the parish can be illuminating or dispiriting, or both together, and the same goes for such clergy gatherings as post-ordination training or deanery meetings. Recent years have seen a number of deanery chapters going away for a few days for common reflection and study. Given the remarkable variety of viewpoints in the Church of England and the strength with which they are held, this might be seen as a recipe for disaster. It is unfortunately true that some deanery chapters do not amount even to being a support group. Yet if there is some notion of the life of the Church as common, of teamwork which is more than

collaboration for collaboration's sake but rooted in a commitment to each other for the sake of Christ, then the diversity can
be an occasion for growth. What may be offered may be understood in different ways – it may even be misunderstood – but
there is always the possibility that a major advance in learning
may take place as a result of things incidental to the matter in
hand, of things not said, or indeed of the simple fact that an
exchange has taken place. Agreement can then arise where it has
not been sensed before. Differences may be uncomfortable, but
they can be occasions for growth and for grace, precisely
because they are uncomfortable. Clearly, learning from each
other's perspectives, gifts and experience will take root only
when it is understood as a common task.

Attitudes

Much of this applies equally to learning and study together with
parishioners. Unseen progress can take place outside any formal
group, where the group has been an important catalyst. The
penny will drop later. In all of this there are two aspects of
Christian life which are often thought to be more at home in the
spiritual life, but belong equally in the community of Christian
study. They are conversion and humility. Conversion is not, by
any standards, a matter of a one-off event that can then be left
behind.

> In any event
>   'Whether at once, as once at a crash Paul
>   Or as Austin, a lingering-out sweet skill'
> being turned towards God is not a coming to standstill.[1]

Conversion in study implies a readiness to be changed
towards the likeness of Christ. It may happen by the study
leading to a change of heart and mind, perhaps as one factor in a
long process, 'a lingering-out sweet skill'. Or it may happen 'as
once at a crash'. It may come about as much through engagement with fellow parishioners as in particular situations. Conversion goes on when strange and not necessarily Christian ideas
are transformed into Christian truth in the mind and heart of the
priest. It will often occur by the trial and test of personal
challenge.

Such a readiness goes hand in hand with humility. This is something which it is fatal to attempt to turn on – it can only come as a gift of God. And yet it is one of those cardinal New Testament gifts which we are called to aspire to. If we approach God as we respond to a person, then we will be talking of study also in terms of gift rather than something we do simply by our own efforts. Before so great a gift as this, humility becomes essential: it is essential for the sharing of it with companions on the same journey; it becomes necessary for its transmission. Indeed, it can be argued that humility is necessary to any authentic rational effort. It is certainly a safeguard of the integrity of the Christian mind and of its readiness for God's truth. This is even more true for those commissioned to serve Christ's people. With the dangers of status, institutionalism and careerism which affect clergy, it is something to be sought all the more. The attitude of humility towards God in worship and prayer is of a part with the same attitude to learning of God in study and interaction.

In addition to the study mentioned above, there is learning for the purposes of study groups, prayer groups, peace and justice groups and so on; or there is learning for the sake of better understanding and celebration of the liturgy. If what has been said about priesthood and the common life of the Church is true, then it is clear that priests learn as much as they communicate; they receive as much as they impart. Often it will go on at levels other than those of the giving and receiving of information. We seek to know God in many ways; some of us employ our gifts to the full, others neglect or misuse them. Many parishioners will not be primarily 'mind' people, but no one would think that prevents them from deepening their under-standing and practice of the faith. Often it will be from people who are no great shakes intellectually that a priest who is a 'mind' person can learn most. A housebound parishioner, struggling with lasting pain and weakness that tests faith to the limit, can, through particular acts or indeed memories thankfully recalled, give to a 'mind-bound' priest a knowledge of the triumph of grace in that person that no reading could yield. Indeed passages of Scripture or of theology may become real for the first time in such circumstances; only then does its life strike home. Equally an area of reflection and study may show up the presence of God in circumstances that seem remote from God's touch, as, for instance, Petru Dumitriu shows in his classic book *To the Unknown God*.

Study and the praying community

None of this process of the sharing of God's truth stands as a purely academic enterprise. Study cannot be separated from the prayer and worship of a parish. If part of the priest's identity lies in nurturing the desire for God and helping others to know the working of God, then study and learning must live in a unity with worship and prayer. The 'law of believing' (*lex credendi*) and the 'law of praying' (*lex orandi*) are not two utterly unconnected items which have been stuffed into the same 'jiffy' bag. Christian life is one, and is given to us in that address of the person of Christ to the persons of Christians, in our case the person of the Christian priest. Many priests to whom academic study comes naturally during training can find the adjustment to parish learning a hard one to make; conversely many who found study hard can take to the parish context like a duck to water. If a college or course has majored on academic study and less on common life and worship, then there are obvious risks to the academically minded priest. Such a division may lead to a similar imbalance in the non-academic priest. Study may get put on the shelf and left there. It seems important that an integral link between study and life be made before ordination. Inevitably, therefore, we are drawn to look at the role study has in a community of those preparing for ordination and how it fits in the future ministry of the priest.

Ordination training as a measuring-rod

Things learnt and studied are not things to be grasped as a private possession but are the stuff of gift, gifts to be shared. Priestly formation exists for the sake of transformation and communication. Believing and praying belong together and are inseparable. The latter gives shape and context to the former, it covers the bones with living flesh; it gives it its very reason for existing. There will often be tensions between one area and another, for instance between worship and the study of doctrine. Not all these tensions will be creative, and there will be times of crisis when unity seems impossible. Even then, in a training community where the life has the right balance the tension will obtain because of an underlying link, not because the two poles are unrelated quantities. The chapel and the library of this institution will not exist as two forces glaring at each other across barricades, for they both belong together. This does not imply any cocooning from intellectual sharpness and questioning. We cannot be excused any of the hard questions. High standards of academic rigour and argument are by rights common to both university and ordination course. There can be no slouching when it comes to these. What is different in the study we describe is the engagement in a common enterprise: it is different in being something not readily found, say, in a university, but it is also study which meshes with a larger common enterprise, which is prayer and liturgy and the life together. In such a course little effort will need to be made to encourage cross-relating of areas of study and experience, for this happens automatically because of the continuous round the clock brewing of the pot.

Christian teaching is a community enterprise

Teaching and practice are passed from mind to mind, soul to soul, person to person; they are not passed down the Church as baton to baton. They are a corporate exercise which involves all Christians all the time (going on in different groupings and at different levels according to circumstances). It is not just the responsibility of synods and councils called now and again to debate matters. It is just as much a feature of the discipleship and struggles of ordinary Christians. We believe by learning from others what they have found out about the love of God, and this is no less true of modern faith communities than it was in the days of St Paul, modern individualism notwithstanding. Christian truth calls for personal engagement; learning in a group with a common goal allows the process of interpretation and response to take place as part of this personal engagement, something which involves all aspects of our response, imaginative, emotional, volitional as well as intellectual. This is particularly so among persons who are conscious of being within a community greater than themselves.

Christian theological study needs to be a community enterprise. If it is not, it will be short on a vital element of experience.

It is also fitting preparation for the same enterprise in the parish, though the study before ordination is likely to be more intense. Indeed, in a restricted sense a college or course can be a church in germ, preparing for the communication and the tensions in parish life which will be very similar. In any such community there are a variety of personal stories and encounters, a variety of skills and abilities, and last but not least failings, blindspots and conflicts. The very practice of study, the marshalling, analysis and use of data at a basic level, will be an alien one, initially forbidding to some. On the other hand the application of study to particular situations, as well as the ability to learn and to be changed by them, will be harder for others. It might appear that this argues for differentiation, for some kind of streaming, but the opposite is in fact the case. While it is undesirable for skills to go without recognition, study and reflection should be a common and shared practice.

Exposure to the challenge posed by other disciplines or outlooks can happen through books, practical exercises, or encounters on placements. More formative still, however, is the exposure to challenges posed by fellow ordinands, which foreshadow the similar challenges in the parish. We are forced to take seriously other people with different characters, histories and failings. And we are allowed no escape from them. If we place importance on the virtues of listening and attention to the other, to what we might call a patient hesitancy, then there arises the possibility of something far more than a group of individuals thrown together who collaborate now and then: there arises the possibility of a community of persons, as opposed to an aggregate of minds, a community of exploration into the truth of God. Such a community will not only be the place where things happen to us, but will be the 'agent' of the whole process of formation and growth. The opportunity for shared experience and reflection becomes a major part of theological study. Engaged community experience is the ideal model of the life of every Christian community, and is a vital vision for the parish. In the setting of training it means that the times between set periods for study are an essential part of the process of learning. It is more than a matter of opportunities for continuing discussion or for seeking assistance from fellow students. It is, as we have said, a vessel in which a brew is constantly going on, whether we are discussing theology or doing the washing-up.

Not just knowledge, but wisdom

Study is much more than the simple acquisition of learning: it meets a person at a particular place and at a particular time, through other persons and their interaction. It involves an understanding of self and past history that are woven in with each other. Our present state is not to be escaped from or anaesthetized; rather is it to be accepted, perhaps revised, and even perhaps converted. Learning also involves unlearning, a movement of undeception within the limitations of our finitude. It involves learning what Christianity does not teach or do, and learning what God is not. When this comes about, the growth in learning does not amount to an increase in knowledge; it is a liberation from something that had deceived or gripped us fast. Such an 'unlearning' is something which happens to us, though we are not purely passive. It is usually painful. Recognition of the limitations of how we receive, learn and pass on is a key to knowing the nature of Christian wisdom.

It follows that the practice of study should foster the making of connections between areas of study. This should be accompanied by discernment in the development of pastoral wisdom. These are most likely to be fostered at depth by ongoing personal interaction. The environment of the common life of the training community will place competing and contrasting demands on time and on emotional resources. Such pressures should not be seen as merely to be endured; they are part of the common learning, occasions for deeper self-knowledge and recognition of the presence of God in the web of such constraints. There will be such competing demands aplenty in later ministry, with many agendas that cannot be seen through to the end.

As has been said a little earlier, there is a necessary link between theology and the rest of the life together. This is crucial because it is not through our own efforts in the library that we construct our own theological language. Rather, the words and concepts are given meaning in our experience of the liturgy, and all our thinking about God is tested and corrected in our prayer and in the tensions (and joys) of common life. The main and essential point is that the concepts and language we use in theological study need to have meaning given to them by the life of the Church – they are not a construct we can arrive at through our own effort.

In prayer and worship the same faith is celebrated and lived in the liturgical action, in relation to the living God. It will go hand in hand with the interplay of question and change, in people coping with their own searchings. Without such living experience of the new life in Christ, the priests-to-be will lack the means to relate their own response to the body of which they are members. They simply will be freelance. They will then lack the ability to arouse in others a thirst for the new life of Christ. What they should be offering to the people of God is the distinctive knowledge of God. For such knowledge there can be no human substitute. It is nothing less than the knowledge of the unknowable God in Christ, the content of life eternal. If they cannot do this they are offering stones for bread.

The study of the ordinand and the priest is engaged theology, one which emerges from the address of Christ, and the response of the one so addressed. The object at the end of study and reflection is not a 'what' or 'that', what God is, or that people have said or done this or that in relation to God. In other words the object of theological study is only knowable through faith informed by love. Here is an open theology; it should be characterized by awareness of the depths and insight of other theological approaches and by a desire to remain open to the mystery of God. A closed mind, one not seeking to surrender itself to the address of God, is the very opposite of the mind that responds to the unknowable God present in Christ. Such a mind should be seeking to surrender the individual and distorted person to Christ, for the sake of formation and transformation by Christ into the mission he gives, the mission of priesthood.

Note

1. Charles Hefling, *Why Doctrines?*, Cambridge, MA: Cowley, 1984, p.35. The quotation is from G.M. Hopkins, 'Wreck of the Deutschland'.

CHAPTER EIGHT

Being a pastor

Andrew Jackson was chaining his bike to the grille over the shop window. He called out cheerfully, 'Hiya, Brian.'

'Hi, Andy,' said Brian with a wink, 'What you doin' goin' into a furniture shop?'

'My mum works here now – didn't you know?'

'Yes, but what you doin' goin' into a furniture shop when you should be at school?'

'Honest, vicar, I wasn't well this mornin' – bit better now.'

'Come for a walk, Andy – bring the bike.'

They set off in the direction of the school. Andy gave him a friendly punch – 'I'll go to school if you let me do thurifer again on Sunday.'

'Not on your nelly – but you can do it at the Paschal Vigil if you go to school every day for the rest of term.'

'Waddya mean – I never miss school!'

'You are today, and you're in enough trouble as it is.'

'What about my poor old mum – you've dragged me away from her.'

'What were you going to see her about?'

'Just goin' to say hello.'

'You can say hello on the way home from school.' He got another amiable punch as Andy went in at the school gate.

No sooner had Brian turned the corner than he bumped into Roger. 'You bearin' fruit?' asked Roger, with the wisdom of the mad.

'Hiya, Roger – givin' me more food for thought, are you?' said Brian.

'Have you got time for a cup of tea?' That was not an invitation – it meant that Brian had to make it. As they sat in the kitchen Roger made people jump every now and then by bellowing things like 'Glory Hallelujah'. Brian was not only good with the mixed-up young – he had an unusual gift for the people others avoided: strange characters, people slightly off their rocker, happy/unhappy eccentrics, seemed to be drawn to him like homing pigeons. Characters in a mess, families who tried the patience of their doctors, their neighbours, and sometimes the police, were to him like congenial and normal friends. He made nothing of it, and even seemed to take pleasure in their oddness and intransigence. He treated them as totally normal people, and often gained their respect for it. No one would have thought he could ever have become a vicar. After some years working in a scrap yard he had moved on to the railways. He stayed at that until his early thirties, when there came to him the thought that he might be a priest. Now here he was in his fifth year at St. Mary's, with Alison as an admirable, if sometimes exasperated, curate.

'Have a nice break, Brian?' said the man in the newsagent's.

'Yes, a whale of a time, thanks, Habib.' A whale of a time particularly on the last day. Half term in a seaside hotel with Janet and the children. Not much to do on the beach in February, but the change was as good as a rest. On the day before they returned they were woken by noises coming through the window.

'I don't know what it's all about,' screamed a woman's voice. 'Leave me, leave me – no, don't go, don't go!' Marjorie, the middle-aged woman in the room next door, was hanging off the balcony. Inside was the manager, trying to get her in before the whole hotel was woken up, and dreading that the police would get involved. It just happened at that moment that Elsie Binns was coming from the loo. Elsie had had a lifetime of hard work, and had the weathered and rock-like face of those who have loved much but made no great fuss about it, quietly slogging on with amazing generosity and common sense. She didn't know what to do – her only qualification was that she had once been a nurse. She went towards the balcony.

'Come on, dear – come and have a cup of tea with me and tell me all about it.' Marjorie came off her perch like a lamb, and allowed herself to be led back into her bedroom.

Now another character appeared on the scene: Joy. She hovered at the closed bedroom door. 'I know all about these cases, I've dealt with plenty of them. I think I'd better go in.'

Brian wasn't convinced. 'Just stay around, love, and see how it goes.'

'She probably doesn't know how to deal with it – I've had the training.' Joy knocked on the door and opened it.

Elsie, with a combination of wavering uncertainty and rock-like firmness which only the meek can display, made sure the door didn't open fully, and said, 'She's a lot quieter now – a cup of tea has done a world of good. She'll be all right now. Thank you very much.'

In the afternoon Brian drove Marjorie to her sister's. 'She's not supposed to go away on her own like that,' she said. 'Perhaps it's time she moved in with me.'

At the Paschal Vigil they were all ready in the vestry to process out and light the New Fire when Andrew came in and whispered: 'Roger's come'. Roger sometimes turned up at church, and they had discovered that if he sat near Brian, Brian had a knack for keeping him quiet, just with a touch or a look. What could they do with him? He would bellow in the dark and give some old dear a heart attack.

'We'll have to make him M.C.,' said Brian with sudden inspiration.

'What's that?' asked Andy.

'Well, he just stands by the vicar and ... keeps an eye on things. Very good thing to have, an M.C.' They got Roger a cassock and surplice, and he was as good as gold through the whole long service, except during one of the silences when, to the delight of the choir children, he bellowed 'Glory be!' as he sat in state, with a voice so stentorian that Alison almost fell off her seat on the other side of Brian.

While they were still celebrating in these unconventional circumstances, over at St Peter's they had just finished, and Kath was standing in the crowd outside the church door lighting up her first paschal fag. Kevin was out for the count – never had he had such an exhausting week – even worse than the vacation job he had once had at Harrod's during the January sales. Reg Keen's much more simple service in the school hall was crawling with children, while the East Botting team had for once got their act together, and shared out the services among the churches. It even looked now as though they were going to be able to salvage the trip to Taizé.

They were all caught up in the night of nights, in which past, present and future become one. The mystery that was in them was not something they could be equipped with – it was intimately part of themselves – just as they were. Or, rather, as they were becoming.

Parish accountant and administrator,
typist and banker, news duplicator,
reference composer and pencil-end biter,
passport endorser, certificate writer.

Digger of garden, inspector of drains,
checking the roof each time that it rains.
Re-designer of churches, re-arranger of pews,
closer of windows, repairer of loos.

Visitor, caller in, knocker on doors
target of tale-spinners, cadgers and bores.
Something to everyone as I'm passing by,
occasionally wondering, 'Just who am I?'[1]

In this reflection on the life of a parish priest John Marshland raises the kind of question that many clergy face from time to time. Amidst the turmoil of a busy day in the parish, it is easy to forget the underlying purpose of the work that has been done, and even to lose any sense of identity. There is a danger that many clergy will attempt to compensate for this loss by training as specialist therapists or counsellors; for in a world which calls for increasing professionalism and technical competence, this kind of specialization entitles them to be thought of as professional people alongside their peers. But a desire for professionalism of this kind risks undermining the very nature of priestly ministry, for professionalism is concerned very much with the work you do and the way you do it, and although we need priests to be competent in their work, priesthood is bound up more with the person you are than with the work you do.

In what follows, we shall attempt to illustrate how the type of training we have described in earlier chapters serves to prepare the priest for pastoral ministry. In particular, we shall show how a concentrated period of theological formation accelerates a process of personal growth and development which continues not just until ordination, but throughout the priest's life. We shall also show how training in specific skills can complement this process of personal formation, but we will show too that such training on its own cannot properly prepare people for priestly ministry.

It is with some caution that we discuss the pastoral work of the priest apart from the totality of priestly life and work. We saw in Chapter 3 the limitations of talking about priesthood in terms of the work a priest does, and dividing pastoral work off into its own distinctive compartment risks perpetuating some of the misunderstanding we highlighted there. In spite of that risk, there is value in focusing on a particular area of priestly life to show how a concentrated period of formation such as we have described might work in practice. In making this kind of artificial distinction, we must bear in mind that the pastoral ministry of a priest is greater than the pastoral work the priest undertakes. This is because the whole of priestly ministry is in fact pastoral ministry. Priests direct their whole lives to building up and caring for the congregations they serve; and as a part of that process, they will of course be built up and cared for by those congregations.

Christian pastoral care

In the last chapter of St John's Gospel, as the risen Christ commissions Simon Peter to take care of his sheep, he asks him three times: 'Simon son of John, do you love me?' It is Peter's love for Jesus which leads him to care for those whom Jesus loves. Simon Peter feeds Christ's sheep out of gratitude for what he has received from his Lord, and that of course is the motivation for all Christian pastoral care. As in the parable of the sheep and the goats (Matt. 25), love for God is shown in practice in love for our neighbour.

Peter is called to care for Christ's sheep: in that sense, being a pastor is a vocation. That is how it is understood in the letter to the Ephesians (Eph. 4.11), where it is listed as one of the various gifts that Christ gives to his Church. As a vocation, pastoral care demands the involvement of the full person, which is why it is so difficult to separate this role from the rest of the priest's life. One person encounters another and cares for that whole person. This is why later in this chapter we speak of the close link between pastoral care and simple practical support. From the description we have given so far, it might be tempting to imagine that all energy flows in one direction within the pastoral relationship. That is far from being the truth, for all pastoral care is a two-way process.

The pastoral care of the Church is often compared with that of other professional support agencies. Although parallels can be drawn, there exists the important distinction that pastoral care within the body of Christ has a primary concern with the spiritual, as well as the physical, welfare of an individual. This is what is implied when we speak of caring for the whole person. Many of the healing miracles in the New Testament remind us of the close connection between physical healing and the forgiveness of sins. If you are caring for the whole person, then there may well be a need to declare that sins are forgiven. There is an Anglo-Saxon liturgy of healing in which the priest is called to shrive, anele and housel his flock. The whole person is healed through the three sacraments of penance, anointing, and communion. In the letter to the Ephesians, ministry is spoken of in terms of 'building up the body of Christ, until all of us come to the unity of the faith and of the knowledge of the Son of God, to maturity, to the measure of the full stature of Christ' (Eph. 4.12f). This is the underlying aim of all Christian pastors, who take total care of the whole people, although that care must often find expression in very practical ways.

Sometimes, building up the body of Christ involves forcing members of that body to stop and consider what they are doing. An important Christian characteristic is a willingness to admit that we do not have all the answers, a preparedness to subject our will to that of God. Discerning the will of God is a lifelong task for us all, but there are of course times when the Church can and does speak in the name of Christ. And it is the bishops and priests who are appointed to do this. So for the sake of good

pastoral care, there are times when priests have to speak in
Christ's name, perhaps confronting presuppositions and beliefs
which they believe to be ill-founded. This works both within the
Christian community, and also within the wider community,
where clergy have sometimes to challenge prevailing social and
political values.

People are free to ignore such comments, but because the
priest speaks with the authority of the Church, many people
take more notice of comments from a priest than they would
from someone else. Although it is sometimes argued that this
gives the priest undue influence over other people, in practice it
usually means that they are burdened with a weight of responsibility from which others are spared.

The influence that the priest has means that caution has to be
exercised, and in today's world, where people are often reluc-
tant to listen to other people's opinions, pastoral guidance of
this kind is usually only effective where a good relationship has
already been built up between priest and people. When advice is
given, it normally requires that the priest first spend a good deal
of time listening to what the other person has to say.

We have already mentioned that pastoral care is sometimes
shown in practical ways. To take up an illustration used earlier
in the book, it may well be that a priest spends time changing
light bulbs for an elderly couple. This serves in part to enable the
priest to get to know the couple, and to build up a relationship
of trust with them. But something more important is at work. If
a couple have no light, then it may well be that at a particular
moment changing a light bulb is the best possible way of
expressing Christ's love for them. This relationship is of course
reciprocal: and members of a congregation frequently perform
practical domestic tasks for their priest. Showing Christ's love to
people is required if all are to 'come to the unity of the faith and
of the knowledge of the Son of God' – but often this love is most
effectively communicated through simple acts of service of this
kind.

In a busy parish, it is easy for practical chores to mount up
and become overwhelming, as their underlying purpose is buried beneath a pile of overdue correspondence. John Marshland's
poem reminds us of a possible consequence: that of losing any
sense of identity. But it is precisely that danger which highlights
the need for a concentrated period of formation which will

provide clergy with a foundation on which to build during the course of their ministry.

Rooted in the liturgy

Recovering a sense of identity does not come from working harder. It is only through our entry into new life with Christ in the Church that we can hope to find ourselves: for who we are is a gift from God. Pastoral care is concerned with helping people find their real selves, for that is to put in other words what we have spoken of in terms of enabling people to come 'to maturity, to the measure of the full stature of Christ'. This is what Jesus describes as having life abundantly (John 10.10). If priests are to be able to help people pastorally, then they need to be people who themselves are seeking to attain to the full stature of Christ. It is not enough simply to have engaged in theological study and debate, for priests cannot hope to help other people engage in a process of which they have no personal experience.

It is for this reason that we have emphasized the central role of the liturgy in ordination training. We are using the word 'liturgy' here as an all-encompassing term. It refers not only to the public worship of the Church, centred on the Sunday Eucharist, and finding expression in morning and evening prayer, and perhaps in a daily Eucharist, but also to private prayer and meditation. Clergy have a responsibility to pray with people. But it is more than a responsibility: it is of course a privilege to be able to be with people at times of distress and celebration, and to help them bring their concerns and their joys to God. Nevertheless, many clergy are hesitant about offering to pray with people, but it is their personal experience of God in the liturgy which will equip them to do so.

As pastors, priests need to do more than simply reiterate what they have learned from books: they need to hand on what they have experienced for themselves. St Paul is emphatic when he tells the Galatians: 'I want you to know, brothers and sisters, that the gospel that was proclaimed by me is not of human origin; for I did not receive it from a human source, nor was I taught it, but I received it through a revelation of Jesus Christ' (Gal. 1.11f). Paul knows that his message will only hold credibility for his readers if they believe that he is speaking from firsthand experience. Today we hear the voice of Christ in the liturgy of the Church, and so it is in the word and sacrament that all training for priesthood must be rooted, for this is where the encounter with Christ takes place. Out of that encounter comes the confidence the priest needs in order to present Christ and his claims to the world.

Speaking from firsthand experience avoids the tendency to be dogmatic, for anyone engaged in the Christian pilgrimage knows that the way is paved with stumbling blocks. It is when priests disclose something of their own journey, and begin to reveal their own weaknesses, that other people can glimpse that this is a journey for them too, and not one which is restricted to the people they think of as spiritual giants.

The common life of the Church

Pastoral care is rooted in the common life of the Church. It is the responsibility of the whole body of Christ, but within the body the priest is called by God to fulfil a particular role: that of making present and representing the person of Christ to his people. For that to be possible, we have already discussed how priests must undertake an authentic quest for encounter with the one whom they are to represent, but equally important is the priest's participation in the common life of the Church. We saw in a previous chapter how the Church is *koinonia*, communion, and how it is only within that communion that priesthood makes sense, and priests begin to understand who they are. It is because of this essential nature of the Church that Christians participate together in a common life.

Although this book is concerned with priestly ministry, we cannot speak of pastoral care without saying something more about the corporate nature of such care. Increasingly, parishes are developing visiting teams and bereavement teams which have a special responsibility for caring for people both within and outside the congregation. In part this is happening because of a decline in the number of clergy, but it is also a response to a growing awareness that pastoral ministry is not a purely priestly prerogative. Pastoral care is the responsibility of the whole body of Christ. St Paul's image of the body rests on his understanding that 'to each is given the manifestation of the Spirit *for the common good*' (1 Cor. 12.7). Within the Church, all are called to minister to one another, though in this common ministry there exists a variety of gifts. These diverse gifts are the possession of the whole Church, and they come together to build up the life of the Church. It is only against this background of shared pastoral responsibility that we can begin to understand priestly pastoral care.

One of the consequences of the personal growth of which we have spoken is that when a priest no longer needs to find a sense of identity from performing endless chores, it becomes possible to let go of much pastoral work so that other people within the Church can perform a role that is properly theirs. The priest then has to work at building up the congregation to be pastors to one another. This requires an ability and desire to recognize pastoral potential in other people which can be drawn out and developed. Such development happens through preaching and specific training, but is often most effectively taught by example.

Living a common life is an essential component of ordination training, where it is experienced in its own right, and where it also foreshadows the common life of the Church in the parish. It is within this common life that pastoral care takes place, and it is by the very nature of the common life that we learn to relate to other people. In our earlier discussion of this subject, it was shown how the common life concentrates the tensions and problems of ordinary life, for when we live in close proximity to others, we cannot avoid being faced both with them and with ourselves. That process changes who we are, and it also helps us learn to live with other people. As we live alongside others, we relate to them in many different ways. Sometimes we challenge or confront them; sometimes we sympathize with them or console them; occasionally we may encourage or inspire them; often we just go about our daily lives simply knowing the other person is there. And any of those processes can be reversed so that where we were giving, we now receive, and the other person gives. Essential for any of this to happen is a willingness for one person to listen to the other.

For a priest to be an effective pastor, it is important to have experienced all these ways of relating to other people. Such experience is more readily available to those students living together in college day in day out than it is to people being trained on one of the courses. However, if it is recognized that this is an essential component of any course, adjustments can be made so that all students can have some experience of living the common life during their training. Moreover, the common life is to be found in places other than shared periods of residence. Students who are training on a course continue to be part of a local Christian community, and it is to be hoped that they experience something of the common life within their own church. This is not always the case, however, for the process of formation normally means that their involvement with their local church is reduced, so that during training the common life is not always part of their experience. Moreover, many Christian congregations live a very shaky common life, sharing perhaps no more than their Sunday morning service. If that is the sole experience ordinands gain of Christian community, they will stand little chance after ordination of being able to build up the common life of the congregations they serve. It is for this reason that it is important for the common life to have been experienced as a part of theological training so that it can be identified and built upon within the parish.

The common life of the family

Most of us have some experience of growing up in a family, and have learned something of what it means to relate to other people in that environment. Ordinands and priests who are married can rightly claim to experience different types of relationship within their daily life. Theological training often fails to take family demands and experience into account, and both partners in the marriage often face considerable emotional and psychological tensions, both during training and subsequently in the parish. Although it is clear in theory that priesthood cannot take precedence over the claims of the marriage, working out what this means in practice is often a very stressful process.

While we cannot attempt here to discuss this issue in any detail, we must bear in mind the important contribution of family life in equipping someone for pastoral ministry. On the other hand, pastoral care within the Church takes place without the specific advantages offered by the family bond. Within a family there is often a shared experience which means that many things are taken for granted, without needing to be spelled out; and families still provide a flexibility, or elasticity, in their relationship, which is uncommon in other circumstances. Within their family, ordinands and priests learn to give and take, but that relationship alone does not necessarily equip them for living within, and building up, the common life of a parish.

Skills to be learned

As 'members of one another' (Eph. 4.25), Christians can surely assume a certain level of mutual trust. However, for pastoral care to be effective, this has to be built up into a relationship of mutual respect, and this requires basic listening and counselling skills on the part of the pastor. Through the experience of living the common life such skills begin to develop naturally, but there are in addition well-established principles and methods for training in such skills, which should be incorporated into theological training. Many colleges and courses also teach other skills to help prepare the ordinand for parish life. There may be some basic psychology, perhaps some instruction in different methods of communication and teaching, and very practical advice about administration, and the use of time. Such teaching can be valuable, but more important than acquiring specific skills is the need for personal growth. Theological training is about more than plugging gaps. It helps an ordinand grow in personal knowledge, and that means becoming aware of weaknesses as well as developing strengths. People engaged in pastoral work need to know their own limits, and be prepared to seek outside help as necessary.

We discussed in Chapter 3 how the priest needs to become a certain kind of person: someone who grows in a particular way into the likeness of Christ. If that process is under way, training in skills promotes growth. On the other hand, without that process, a course which is designed to do no more than impart skills risks producing nothing but a non-directive counsellor, whose mention of God may be thought intrusive, and who has nothing of the authenticity that comes from experiencing Christ in the liturgy, nor any of the understanding of self and of others that is the product of sharing in the common life of the Church.

A bag of tools

Of course no period of priestly formation, whether full-time in a college or part-time on a course, can hope to provide the student with more than a bag of tools to tackle the pastoral problems that will be encountered in parish life. During training students can only begin to familiarize themselves with these tools. It is throughout the course of their priestly ministry that they will learn to sharpen them and use them more effectively. If, as we have suggested, the most important part of preparing for ordination is the personal growth of the ordinand, ordination training has to give shape to a process which enables that to happen. Many students long to be given the manual that tells them which tools to use for which problem, but training cannot produce master craftsmen, nor supply ready-made kits for each problem. A proper balance of personal formation and training in skills can produce people with the potential to be pastors. They have to write the manual themselves in the light of their own experience; but the people they are serving will have quite a lot of influence on the contents of such a manual.

In order for someone to develop their pastoral potential, practical experience is essential. Some people begin formation after many years of such experience. For them, it is important that their experience is acknowledged, and that their training is flexible enough to provide for theological reflection on their past. Often this does not happen, and people feel that their previous life counts for nothing. This risks making the ordinand feel undervalued, and deprives the Church of an important resource.

Some people have had relatively little relevant experience, but during training practical experience is gained in the course of pastoral placements. The student spends time in a parish, and in other attachments – perhaps with a chaplain in a hospital or a prison, or with the Samaritans, or with an Industrial Mission Team. Placements of this kind enable students to see other people carrying out expert care in a variety of situations, and try it themselves under supervision. Students learn to use their pastoral tools in the same way that an apprentice carpenter might stand at the end of the bench and watch the master at work. Little by little, they pluck up the courage to try for themselves. Placements build up a student's confidence, and provide for supervised reflection on the experience. In this way, general principles are learned which will be of benefit when carried over later into parish life.

Inevitably, there is something artificial about pastoral placements, but they do allow privileged access to a wide variety of pastoral situations which are not readily experienced in the normal course of life.

Moving into the parish

The way of life which undergirds the period of formation does not come to an end with ordination. It is in the parish that this pattern is built upon and developed, as it is tested and applied day by day. The experience of common life during training establishes principles for parish life, though in today's increasingly fragmented society they are principles which need to be translated into a language appropriate for local circumstances. If the Church is indeed *koinonia*, and not just a group of like-minded people who come together more or less haphazardly to collaborate over a particular project, then it is a body made up of a wide variety of people with different gifts and various needs. Although those people who make up the Church in any particular place may be dispersed over a fairly wide area, they need to share some kind of common life together. In training this life was focused on corporate worship, and it is firstly as a worshipping community that a local church lives out its distinctive vocation. But another important component of this life together is the daily table, especially at times of celebration for the community or individuals within that community, and meals together are an important ingredient in parochial life. Though the way of life in most parishes is less structured than during the training period, the experience of the course or college has to establish a foundation which can now be built upon.

It is within the common life of the parish, rooted in corporate and personal prayer, that the formation of the priest (and of all the members of the church) continues. During the period of training, the student gained some practical experience in the course of placements, and previous experience and skills took on a new meaning and relevance. It is in the first curacy that what we have called pastoral potential is developed or shattered, for here the newly ordained deacon is faced with a wide range of pastoral needs. In the attempt to meet some of these needs, skills of empathy, sympathy, and distancing should develop, as well as an awareness of the ways in which it is possible to bear one another's burdens. Since it is by interaction with people that experience is acquired, it is to a large extent the people of the parish who enable a curate's pastoral potential to be worked out in practice.

One important aspect of pastoral care of which we have made no mention so far is preaching. In one of his sermons, St Gregory the Great claims: 'It is for love of him that I do not spare myself in preaching him.' This reminds us that preaching, like all pastoral care, is part of our response to God for his great love to us.

As part of a priest's pastoral ministry, we may define the purpose of preaching as 'building up the body of Christ, until . . . all come to . . . the measure of the full stature of Christ' (Eph. 4.12f). Preaching is an important part of the common life of a church, and has to flow from the experience of living within that common life. This means that the primary place for learning to preach is the parish. Ground rules and some experience can be provided during training, but it is only possible to gain real experience of preaching when it becomes a part of the regular pastoral work of the priest. Harry Williams CR tells of this need to preach from experience in his book, *True Wilderness*:

> I resolved that I would not preach about any aspect of Christian belief unless it had become part of my own life-blood. For I realized that the Christian truth I tried to proclaim would speak to those who listened only to the degree in which it was an expression of my own identity.[2]

So it is that the capacity for preaching will mature and change during the course of a priest's ministry as personal growth takes place. But with that increase in the priest's capacity for preaching, there should come too some development in the congregation, and perhaps a greater receptivity to what is being said.

What has been said about learning to preach within the context of the local church is also true of the occasional offices: baptisms, weddings, and funerals. Again it is possible as part of the training period to discuss underlying principles, but it is only in conducting these occasional offices in the parish that the appropriate approach can be learned. If baptism is about becoming a member of the Church, how that is to be experienced and communicated depends to a large extent on the nature of the common life in any particular parish. With all these occasional offices, the people taking part may have little regular contact with the life of the Church. For that reason, the representative nature of the priest comes to the fore, as the priest is seen to speak on behalf of the local Christian community. Of course it is important that the community is represented as often as possible by a variety of people and not just the priest.

With the occasional offices, the underlying purpose of priestly care remains constant. Being an effective pastor in these circumstances requires a humble recognition that this is holy ground, where Christ's presence may be known. It requires a willingness to speak of God, and a readiness to hear him speaking. So again we are reminded that all pastoral care is a two-way process, for pastors gain as much as they give, and have to approach their work with a profound gratitude to God for revealing himself to them in the people they meet.

Training and supervision in the parish

It will be realized that the first curacy is extremely important, for it is here that a great deal of practical fine-tuning takes place. Training and supervision for the first curacy are left largely in the hands of the training incumbent. Because training does not end with ordination, but continues in the parish, all those who are responsible for training newly ordained deacons need to be trained themselves. Being a parish priest is not sufficient preparation to train others, and much more attention needs to be given to how training incumbents might be equipped for this important task.

In practice, even at present, there are many cases where the first curacy works well, but there are also too many instances of a breakdown in relations between a curate and incumbent. A diocese could usefully provide some kind of consultant to help facilitate this relationship. Over the years, the nature of the relationship has changed, and perhaps grown in intensity as the number of curates in many parishes has reduced. The pressures can be considerable. Vicar and curate have to co-operate as colleagues, but are also expected to work together at many other levels. They share together their life of prayer; they respond jointly to difficult pastoral problems; and there is often the additional assumption (by them and by others) that some bond of friendship must also exist. The strains produced by these expectations might be relieved if a disinterested consultant were on hand with whom it were possible to discuss the tensions of the relationship. This would be most advantageous as a preventative measure. It is bound to be less effective when a consultant is brought in only when the relationship is already foundering.

An alternative solution would be to extend the training network for the newly ordained curate. Post-ordination training currently varies considerably among dioceses, but often has no perceptible sense of direction or purpose. It would improve considerably if it were able to provide a means of spreading the responsibility for pastoral supervision of the new curate. This might have the disadvantage, however, of unsettling further those incumbents who had been made to feel vulnerable by the arrival of a lively and talented young curate.

Reflection upon pastoral work with a supervisor helps consolidate the lessons learned. This is possible if the incumbent is a good pastor, but much more difficult when the incumbent's skills and priorities lie elsewhere, or where the relationship between the incumbent and curate is delicate. To solve this problem, some people attempt to shift the responsibility for pastoral training back to the pre-ordination period. This is not the answer, for it is only through honest and regular critical assessment that skills grow, and the primary setting for that to happen must be the parish. An alternative solution, such as those we have suggested, has to be found.

Another option?

There is a current tendency in the Church of England to want to change the whole method of formation. An example is given in an appendix to the recent report on theological training, *A Way Ahead*. In this, Canon Joy Tetley proposes that an ordinand's primary locus of training should be the parish. This would involve a longer period in the first parish, including two years before ordination to the diaconate. Within the training period, certain blocks of time would be spent on concentrated study at a Regional Theological Centre. Canon Tetley's proposal contradicts the thesis of this book, since it fails to realize the need for formation, concentrating instead on preparation for the tasks of pastoral ministry. It also fails to recognize the limitations of the training relationship between incumbent and curate. To place greater strains on this relationship reveals a lack of caution which we should not wish to encourage. Few parish clergy are likely to have all the qualities required to give what was formerly provided around the clock by a college.

Of course the parish plays a vital part in training, since it is primarily (but not exclusively) in the parish that the priest is destined to live and work. We too have placed great emphasis on the training which takes place in the parish, but there is of course a fundamental difference between this new approach and our own. For in our model of theological training, an initial intensive period is required in which the ordinand begins to grow into the kind of person a priest is called to be. Only when the guidelines for that process have been laid down, and a pattern of life is established, can growth continue in the parish. And an important contribution to this growth comes from sharing the daily common life of the parish, during which practical pastoral skills are learned and fine-tuned.

Recent proposals omit all discussion of the need for personal growth, and tend rather to adopt a method which is concerned exclusively with the acquisition of skills. This approach implies an understanding of priesthood as a job with tasks to be performed.

The whole thrust of this book is that priesthood is more than a job, and the Church is more than a club. For the body of Christ is a sacrament, through which God in Christ is present in the world, and within that body, God calls priests to be a focus, a witness and an encouragement to his people. In that sense, priestly life is both sacramental and pastoral. To be good pastors, priests need to develop their pastoral potential. At the beginning of this chapter we mentioned the danger of trying to discuss pastoral ministry in isolation from the rest of priestly ministry. To attempt to teach pastoral skills in isolation is to make that same mistake. Such skills have to be learned, but this is possible only as an integrated part of priestly formation.

Notes

1. Quoted in M. Casey, *What are we at?*, Dublin: Columba Press, 1992, p.183.
2. H.A. Williams, *True Wilderness*, London: Constable 1965, p.8.

CHAPTER NINE

Shaping the shepherds

There is tremendous preoccupation today with what you have rather than who you are. This is as true of training for ordination as it is in other fields. There is a mounting preoccupation with qualifications, pieces of paper and skills. The picture of priesthood painted in this book is not an alternative to that, but the completion of the picture. Qualifications and skills are necessary, but even more important is the kind of persons we are.

Many excellent deacons and priests are being ordained today in the Church. However, of the good things that are happening, many are haphazard and peripheral. We have lost, as a Church, a firm grasp on the essential character of Church, priesthood and formation as outlined in this book. This ought to be right in the middle of the Church's life, at its very foundations. If it is not solidly there in the foundations, then the whole structure will become increasingly shaky, however good particular parts of it remain. Many parishes are lively and full of hope, but unfortunately they are not the whole picture. The state of the clergy themselves is far from rosy. Many people, whatever their views on, say, the ordination of women, or on ecumenism or liturgy, have an unnerving sensation that the foundations might be turning bit by bit from stone to sand.

The formation of the priests of the future will determine the nature of the Church. We do not seem to be aware of how crucial ordination training is to the Church's future. The extent of the danger is made clear in the following account by Helmut Steinlein of the current situation in the 'Lutheran' Church in Germany (Steinlein is an experienced ecumenist and parish priest in Munich). That the situation has implications for more than the Church becomes clear in his account. Mistakes in formation are not just a matter of detail: they damage the Church in its entirety and so weaken its witness to the world.

(Translator's note: *evangelisch* has been translated 'Lutheran', and *evangelikal* as 'Evangelical', as these two interpretations are immediately understandable by English readers.)

A young theology student recently said to me, 'Theological study has as its aim the quest for God, but many students lose him completely, rather than find him.' Even if this is not universally true, these words reflect closely enough the difficult situation in theological study in Germany. What lies behind it?

The situation of the students

Not everyone who studies theology has the intention of seeking God, even if certainly for most of them there is (in the broadest sense) a religious interest. Many understand their future calling as before all else a social activity. They want to improve the world, and see themselves as helpers of humanity, psychological counsellors, and political activists. Often these students come from non-church families, and have little or no contact with their home parish community. Even during study they do not go to church very often, and treat the Bible not as a book to be lived, but only as an object of study. The meaning of ordained office as priestly service, and the significance of ordination as consecration for this service is for most theology students unknown and is on the whole not discussed, even during their time of study. Obligatory courses in liturgy, prayer and spirituality (e.g. introduction to retreats) are needed urgently, but the leadership of the Lutheran Church does next to nothing in this area, and optional invitations to such things (e.g. by Lutheran religious orders) are hardly given a moment's thought by the students.

Church and theology

Since the Enlightenment in the eighteenth century there has been in Germany a division between Church and theology. Often theology was understood only as an academic discipline like all the others, but this was not enough to train properly formed pastors or priests for the Church. Of course there were always individual professors (particularly in Evangelical circles) who also concerned themselves with the spiritual formation of their students, but these unfortunately were an exception. The unity of common life, prayer and study, such as has been the tradition of English theological colleges, was still to be found in Germany in the sixteenth and seventeenth centuries, but after that was swept away.

Enormous difficulties were created by the close integration of theology faculties in the state universities during the Third Reich, as the Nazis made their influence closely felt even here, in the desire to make future clergy follow their line, or to exclude students who were unacceptable. Such influence was of course impossible in the Roman Catholic seminaries. Dietrich Bonhoeffer at that time began in the seminary of the 'Confessing Church' in Finkenwalde (Brandenburg) to restore the lost unity between common life, prayer and study. One reflection of this experience was his little book *Life Together*.

After the Second World War there arose out of the difficult experiences of the Nazi period church high schools near many theology faculties, either as new foundations or as re-foundations (e.g. in Berlin and Wuppertal). These tried to organize life and study on Bonhoeffer's model, taking as their aims a close relationship with a lively parish community, active experience of mission and ministry, and early steeping in the liturgy of the Church, in order to come to know Scripture and faith in their basic significance for study and future office. However, the theological liberalism which predominates today in Germany has changed much in these high schools for the worse, and caused the original intentions to be ineffective. Quite otherwise is the situation in the seminaries of the Roman Catholic Church: they give their students much greater opportunity to connect their academic study with experience of liturgy and spirituality.

Hopes for the future

Any spiritual renewal of the Lutheran churches and parishes in Germany must presuppose also a renewal of theological study; that is, the creation of a connection between academic study and common life, regular daily office and celebration of the Eucharist, Bible study groups and lectures on spirituality. The colleges of the Church of England appear to us here as a shining example (and any who would attempt to mitigate or abolish them should be warned by our German experience). Even if we in Germany cannot adopt exactly this form of college, we need to have the possibility of theology students in university towns living together in small or larger groups, leading a spiritual life (with common prayer and Eucharist). There are examples in the 'J.A.Bengel-Haus' in Tübingen, and the house of the 'Martin-Luther-Bund' in Erlangen.

This kind of spiritual formation of young ordinands would without doubt counteract the 'head-stuff' of their studies and help prepare them for liturgical service, pastoral work and their life as clergy. In Evangelical circles (until now just about the only quarter with any spiritual approach) a more ecumenical and Catholic attitude could also begin to grow.

Karl Rahner once said: 'The religious person of the future will either be one who has experienced something, or he will no longer exist.' The coming decades will probably present the German Church with great problems (lapsing of believers, possible abolition of the church tax, etc.). Many ask religious questions, and many young people are looking for religious experience, and the answers the Church gives often leave them unsatisfied. So a new generation of priests is urgently needed who will be rooted in the tradition of the One Holy Church, but who, being open to people's questions and needs, will be able to give new answers for a new age, responses which emerge from the Word of God and their own spiritual experience. Academic study is not enough for that. What is needed is a unity of study, life and prayer, an immersion in 'struggle and contemplation', as Roger Schütz of Taizé has said.

Roman Catholic formation for ordination has been mentioned, and the forms it has taken in past and present are of no small interest. Cecily Boulding of Ushaw College writes:

———————

Residential seminaries in the Catholic Church originated with the Council of Trent. Conscious that the low standard of learning and morality among the clergy was one of the scandals that provoked the sixteenth-century Reformation, the Council decreed that, as far as possible, seminaries must be established in connection with 'every cathedral and metropolitan church . . . to educate . . . boys . . . in religion and train them in ecclesiastical discipline'. These provisions covered the outward demeanour of tonsured clerics, who must already be able to read and write, and their training in grammar, music, mathematics and other useful arts as a prelude to their study of 'Scripture, ecclesiastical books, the homilies of saints, the administration of the sacraments and liturgy'. The students were to attend Mass daily, confess their sins monthly and receive communion frequently at the discretion of their confessor. Bishops were to institute 'frequent visitation' to ensure punishment of the disobedient and incorrigible and 'to foster the advancement of so pious and holy an institution'. Detailed indication was given of the resources to be devoted to the construction of the buildings, the salaries of instructors and servants, the maintenance of the students and other necessary expenses.[1]

The Tridentine seminaries served the Church well. Indeed while it was impossible at that date to train Catholic priests in England, the English seminaries at Douai, Rome, Valladolid and Lisbon produced literally hundreds of priests eager to exercise their mission in this country, knowing full well that torture and death awaited them when they were caught. Nevertheless, overhaul of the system was more than due by 1965 when the Second Vatican Council turned its attention to the training of priests.[2] Far from undervaluing the residential character of the seminary this overhaul deepened and enriched the whole concept in the light of a renewed appreciation of the community of the Church. The ministration of priests has as its aim that 'the whole redeemed city, that is the whole assembly and community of the saints should be offered as a universal sacrifice to God through the High Priest who offered himself in his passion, that we might be the body of so great a head'.[3] The perception of the Church as the *People of God*, in which the 'riches of the Christian tradition are currently embodied',[4] is dwelt on at length in all the documents concerning priestly formation which have appeared since the Second Vatican Council,[5] since it is the 'mission of the Church to bring all people into that communion (*koinonia*) of the loving unity enjoyed within the Trinity'.[6]

'The whole programme of priestly formation should be seen as a journey of faith undertaken within the Christian community.'[7] Thus, though it must not be thought of as 'a hermitage cut off from the world',[8] the seminary itself must foster a sense of community: 'Community living should offer the students an enriched experience of Christ in shared life and worship'.[9] This community, however, remains in close contact with the wider community of both Church and world. Theological studies are structured with direct relevance to the concerns of the contemporary world. Students are trained for team work and collaboration with lay folk, both members of the Catholic Church and all those others in whose ministries they will share in some way. In turn some opportunities for suitable theological or ministerial training for others besides ordinands are provided in seminaries, while qualified people from the wider community share in aspects of the ordinands' training and in assessment of their suitability for ordination.

The present emphasis is on an holistic personal formation and not merely on the acquisition of skills. The key theme in the seminary programme is that of integration,[10] and programmes are co-ordinated with this end in view. The different academic disciplines, the pastoral programme, spiritual formation and community life, all contribute in a coherent manner to the students' personal growth in Christ. Liturgical study as well as liturgical prayer acts as a powerful integrating factor in the whole programme. As spiritual formation is thus closely associated with academic and pastoral formation, it is hoped that everything learned is internalized as part of the process of growing in Christian maturity.

Such overall integration can be more satisfactorily achieved in a residential seminary where the community life is itself a formative influence. Assessment must be made of the candidate's freedom of choice and intention, his spiritual, moral and intellectual fitness and progress, his physical and mental health and his capacity to understand the obligations of the priesthood. Rector, staff and students should therefore form a 'family', where students can receive personal attention within a supportive community.[11] 'The whole programme of the seminary should be so organized that, with its atmosphere of piety and silence and its concern for mutual co-operation, it should already be an initiation to the students' future life as priests.'[12]

Since the Catholic Church in the West at present only ordains celibate men, the brotherhood of priests among themselves is a vital support to their vocation and ministry. The seminary provides the seedbed for the development of mature and lasting relationships which will be consecrated by ordination into the *presbyterium* – that brotherhood of diocesan priests around their own diocesan bishop.

Formation is a lifelong process. 'Priests are warned by the bishop at ordination that they are to be *mature in knowledge* and that their teaching should be *spiritual medicine for the People of God*.'[13] This demands ongoing formation which must include direction as an aid to spiritual growth, and continued meditation on Scripture as well as the study of both theology and contemporary culture and science. Post-ordination formation is seen as starting with the diaconate programme, which is designed to ease the transfer from seminary to diocesan ministry, and worked out through close co-operation between seminary staff and bishops, or diocesan vocation directors. Similarly, attempts are made to provide support and opportunities for reflection for the newly ordained priest in his first few years. He is also encouraged to remain in contact with staff and fellow former students at the seminary. It is incumbent on diocesan bishops to make organized provision for periods and occasions of renewed study for their priests throughout life, but it is also the obligation of every priest to recognize his need for this, and seek ways of meeting that need. Exchanges between seminaries, both in this country and abroad, can provide suitable stimulus and opportunity; these are encouraged by the National Episcopal Conference. The Episcopal Conference also recognizes the need to provide suitable training in the appropriate expertise before asking priests to take up specialist ministries, such as specific chaplaincies, not only for their better fulfilment, but also to help those concerned to integrate the new role into their overall priestly vocation.

———————

 We have given some of our attention to processes of formation for ordination, and have done this believing that it tells us something about the life and ministry of the priest in the parish. Whether we look at the one or the other, the message is the same: a whole integrated life founded in the conviction that Christ stands at the centre, and is to be known within the unity of liturgy, ministry and common life, both within the Church, and in its encounter with the people who make up the society to which it belongs. This vision stands at the heart of this book, so much so that the reader may feel some surprise that other important questions have not been touched on. We have not, however, aimed to be comprehensive – many significant areas have been left out of account, for reasons of space and for clarity.

In these times of weakness of faith, and in a society as secularized as ours, the Church needs its priests to have had a strong experience of worshipping community and common life during their formation if they are to be agents of community and the knowledge of God. Ordinands come from settings where 'piety' is weaker and patchier than ever before, and are in need of what often amounts to a spiritual conversion. They also come from a life where experience of community, real community which bites, has not been a great part of their experience, if at all. This ministerial formation is the only opportunity most of them will ever have to experience such things with this particular intensity. It is for them, and for all people who look to the Church for some signpost in the business of being human and in the quest for God, that we have been moved to write this book.

Notes

1. Council of Trent, Session 22, 11.11.1563: *Directions for establishing seminaries for clerics*; see H.J.Schroeder OP, *Canons and Decrees of the Council of Trent*, Illinois: Tan Books, 1978.
2. cf. Roman Catholic Bishops' Conference of England and Wales, *Charter for Priestly Formation*, 1990, pp. 54f.
3. Augustine, *De Civ.Dei* 10.6; quoted in Vatican II, *Presbyterium ordinis*, n.2.

4. *Charter*, p.39.
5. cf. *Charter*, Appendix.
6. *Charter*, p.8.
7. *Charter*, p.41.
8. Congregation for Catholic Education, *Ratio fundamentalis*, 1985, p.217.
9. *Charter*, p.67.
10. cf. Vatican II, *Optatam totius*, nn. 15–16 and notes.
11. *Optatam totius*, nn. 5, 7.
12. *Optatam totius*, n. 11.
13. *Presbyterium ordinis*, n. 19.

CHAPTER TEN

Three encounters

It was evening. Candles glowed in front of icons; here and there dark forms breathed quietly in the still darkness. Then someone very quietly read a psalm. Silence again, with a low hum of distant traffic. All of a sudden there was the sound of breaking glass. Loud banging started at the doors. They had thought the church was all shut up, and were having a go at it, unaware that something called Evensong was going on inside by the light of a candle or two.

Chris reacted with an ironic humour which was now habitual. You had to laugh at these kids. 'Typical – trying to kick the door down when all they had to do was turn the knob. They wouldn't think to see if it was locked.'

The priest had a way of talking about the antics of the locals that might make it all seem hilarious, except that you could detect a tension behind the humour.

A group of youths outside were so taken by surprise by Chris's appearance that for a split second they just stared; then they ran off hell for leather. Chris knew them well, and was respected by them. And yet there were inexplicable occasions such as now when it came upon them to have a go at the church. This place dragged out of you a monumental patience and perseverance – quite a revolution for someone who was so impatient. It was exhilarating, but it tested you to the limit. They had started a youth club, and that said it all. The kids wanted it, enjoyed it, and yet did things which were such a kick in the teeth that it seemed mad to carry on. They simply did not understand. They were oblivious. Thoughts like that sometimes flashed through the mind and then disappeared. The truth lay not there, in fact, but in a grinding together of seeming irreconcilables which was like the birth-pangs of creation. You could not help liking them, particularly those who are the worst. You even found yourself defending people who were little more than thugs when they were criticized at meetings. It was full of paradox.

'Why haven't these gone out yet?' Chris asked Carol the churchwarden, pointing to a pile of leaflets on the vestry floor advertising the church fair, a new venture which was making a rickety and uncertain progress.

'I thought they had,' she replied, with what seemed a suitable astonishment.

Chris carried a pile out of the room. 'Bill and Irene had said they were going to get them out in good time.'

'I'll help you do it,' said Carol, who, with her large family, could hardly spare the time. There was no point in saying anything about the way people let you down. 'People aren't used to organizing things like this,' said Carol, laughing. It didn't make them any less generous and warm-hearted. There was simply something that had yet to be learnt about being dependable.

In amongst everybody and everything there always stood the icons, the people, the altar. These three images for Chris showed up the holiness of this unloved estate, even the holiness of kicking down a church door. The saints in the icons were not too proud to muck in. The congregation were valiant, salt of the earth, and the altar spoke of the daily recitation of the Scriptures and the mysteries. It meant that it was possible to laugh as well as to gripe. It was possible to stay serene and get on with it.

There was something about this which affected the others too, Bill and Irene, Carol, and many others. Christ became present in the daily bread of the streets littered with broken glass, and the youths 'doing' a house, the shops behind metal grilles, and the warm and welcoming homes.

Chris was preparing a sermon to preach at the ordination in a

138

neighbouring cathedral. Inevitably it came out of life on the estate. Three things emerged: incomprehension, unreliability, and worship. Three stories from the Gospels would not go away.

Meanwhile Bill and Irene had now excelled themselves. They may have been bad at organizing urgent deliveries of leaflets, but it now turned out that they had done something else which had never happened in that congregation before. They had heard that Marjorie had had a stroke and was in hospital. They saw her at church, but hardly knew her. But they had bought a bunch of flowers and got on a bus and gone to see her. Those were the small signs of resurrection which made it almost comic to complain. You would be busy blaming people, only to have the carpet then completely swept out from under your feet.

The following extract from Chris's ordination sermon appeared in the diocesan newspaper:

> There are three stories in the Gospels which echo amongst themselves, and they have something to say about the mystery of being a priest. They are three stories of encounter. The first is the transfiguration. Christ takes the disciples off to an encounter which is incomprehensible to them. There on the top of the mountain they simply do not understand. As often happens in moments of acute embarrassment, they blurted out a silly suggestion which completely missed the point. One thing the priest has to learn is that incomprehension is a two-way matter. We clergy may complain that people do not understand, but that assumes we do understand, when very often it is clear that we understand so little. Where the ferment of life is carrying forward the miracle of God's creation there may be very little we can understand at all. It may all be paradox and struggle, and yet we can be driving around the parish and find ourselves saying to our constant surprise, 'It is good to be here'.
>
> The second story is Gethsemane. The whole passion narrative shows a monumental case of being let down, and Gethsemane is the place where this awful truth first becomes stark. Just as on the mount of transfiguration, the disciples fall asleep. They are

hopeless – no idea of what is required of them. Christ simply takes them as they are. Dependability is something that just has to be learnt. This too is a two-way matter. Both priest and people are undependable, unprofitable servants. There are many people whom we cannot see whom we let down without being aware of it. There is a great danger for the priest in coming to see the parish in us-and-them terms, however benign they may be: the priest and Christ on the one side, and the people on the other. The priest and Christ together have to teach the people. This thought lurks all the time, bending our minds away from the real truth: we are all caught up together in the Fall, we learn from each other, we find Christ in each other, we are redeemed through each other, most specially when things happen which we don't understand. The priest can be like the starter switch in a neon light. Without the priesthood, the whole process of the Christian life becomes vitiated and bland. One of the priest's distinctive functions is to set things going – this is done first by what you are rather than what you can plan. What you are will set people on fire, if you are faithful to Christ's particular call. The transfiguration points to the cross, and Gethsemane brings us close enough for the discomfort to be acute. They issue in the third story, that of the two disciples on the road to Emmaus.

These two travellers were like people who have been blindfolded. The crucifixion had left them disoriented and aimlessly wandering all over the place. The beginning may be full of hope. But there will be setbacks on the way that can be so great as to drain us of all courage. These two travellers had had all their enthusiasm demolished. And yet soon they would be hurrying back along the road in very different mood, for by then they had known Christ again. The first calling of priests in the Church of God is to follow Christ and to know him. It is in knowing him that the whole matter with which they have to do is grounded. For it is not they who visit, heal, strengthen, teach and shepherd, but it is Christ himself who does these things in them. In the breaking of the bread Christ set something off in these two people. At the Eucharist the Body of Christ encounters itself and discovers itself by knowing the Lord. The fruits may be humble – a bunch of flowers taken to someone we don't know in hospital, or a priest who has learned a little generosity and patience. But they are signs of greater things to come.

All three of these stories also apply to priesthood in a different way, by showing the priest's function of being a sacramental presence of Christ, a presence among presences. The priest is to lead people to things which at first seem difficult to comprehend, but they follow because they see something of the transfigured Christ in their priest. Every priest also pays visits to Gethsemane, and passes through moments of crucifixion. In presiding at the breaking of the bread these mysteries find their root and their fountain of life for both priest and people. The priest as catalyst lives a distinctive and particular life. Priesthood belongs within various fields of gift which set each other off. Like two colours in a painting, or two comedians in a double act. The current fashion for talking about general purpose 'ministry' is ill thought out and will exhaust itself, for it ignores the sacramental nature of the body of Christ. Christians can have no interest in hierarchies of gift or degrees of gift. The differences are more dynamic than mere differences of degree or rank. They are, rather, like the relationship between the arts. Between music to be heard, and painting to be seen, for instance. We all need each other. The body of Christ is more than a mere conglomerate of well meaning co-operation and mutual appreciation. Its life is a dynamic interaction of differences. It is clay taken over by fire.

Kath straightened her 'ordination hat'. 'This has two years on, one year off,' she said with a mischievous smile, 'a deaconing, a priesting, and then a fallow year.'

'I liked the sermon very much,' said Mr Hill, 'full of good things.'

'Bit too hifalutin' for me,' said Kath, 'but then we're all different. It's the differences that make life a teaser, isn't it? I like teasers.'